# How to Know the Ferns

## A GUIDE

### TO THE NAMES, HAUNTS, AND HABITS OF
### OUR COMMON FERNS

By

Frances Theodora Parsons

*Author of "How to Know the Wild Flowers,"*
*"According to Season," etc.*

Illustrated by

Marion Satterlee and Alice Josephine Smith

*SECOND EDITION*

Dover Publications, Inc.
New York

Published in Canada by General Publishing Company, Ltd., 30 Lesmill Road, Don Mills, Toronto, Ontario.

Published in the United Kingdom by Constable and Company, Ltd., 10 Orange Street, London WC 2.

This Dover edition, first published in 1961, is an unaltered republication of the original work with the omission of six photographic illustrations. These illustrations contributed little to the value of the work and were omitted because of their poor quality. The work was originally published by Charles Scribner's Sons in 1899.

*Standard Book Number: 486-20740-4*
*Library of Congress Catalog Card Number: 61-1261*

Manufactured in the United States of America
Dover Publications, Inc.
180 Varick Street
New York, N. Y. 10014

TO

J. R. P.

"*If it were required to know the position of the fruit-dots or the character of the indusium, nothing could be easier than to ascertain it; but if it is required that you be affected by ferns, that they amount to anything, signify anything to you, that they be another sacred scripture and revelation to you, helping to redeem your life, this end is not so easily accomplished.*"

—THOREAU

# PREFACE

Since the publication, six years ago, of " How to Know the Wild Flowers," I have received such convincing testimony of the eagerness of nature-lovers of all ages and conditions to familiarize themselves with the inhabitants of our woods and fields, and so many assurances of the joy which such a familiarity affords, that I have prepared this companion volume on " How to Know the Ferns." It has been my experience that the world of delight which opens before us when we are admitted into some sort of intimacy with our companions other than human is enlarged with each new society into which we win our way.

It seems strange that the abundance of ferns everywhere has not aroused more curiosity as to their names, haunts, and habits. Add to this abundance the incentive to their study afforded by the fact that owing to the comparatively small number of species we can familiarize ourselves with a large proportion of our native ferns during a single summer, and it is still more surprising that so few efforts have been made to bring them within easy reach of the public.

I wish to acknowledge my indebtedness to the many books on our native ferns which I have consulted, but more especially to Gray's "Manual," to Eaton's "Ferns of North America," to the "Illustrated Flora" of Messrs. Britton and Brown, to Mr. Underwood's "Our Native Ferns," to Mr. Williamson's "Ferns of Kentucky," to Mr. Dodge's "Ferns and Fern Allies of New England," and to that excellent little quarterly, which I recommend heartily to all fern-lovers, the "Fern Bulletin," edited by Mr. Clute.

To the State Botanist, Dr. Charles H. Peck, who has kindly read the proof-sheets of this book, I am indebted for many suggestions; also to Mr. Arthur G. Clement, of the University of the State of New York.

To Miss Marion Satterlee thanks are due not only for many suggestions, but also for the descriptions of the Woodwardias.

The pen-and-ink illustrations are all from original drawings by Miss Satterlee and Miss Alice Josephine Smith.

In almost all cases I have followed the nomenclature of Gray's "Manual" as being the one which would be familiar to the majority of my readers, giving in parentheses that used in the "Illustrated Flora" of Messrs. Britton and Brown.

FRANCES THEODORA PARSONS

ALBANY, March 6, 1899

*" The more thou learnest to know and to enjoy, the more full and complete will be for thee the delight of living."*

# CONTENTS

# CONTENTS

# LIST OF PLATES

*₊* *The actual sizes of ferns are not given in the illustrations.  For this information see the corresponding description.*

# LIST OF PLATES

# LIST OF ILLUSTRATIONS

## LIST OF ILLUSTRATIONS

How to Know the Ferns

New York Fern

# — FERNS AS A HOBBY

I THINK it is Charles Lamb who says that every man should have a hobby, if it be nothing better than collecting strings. A man with a hobby turns to account the spare moments. A holiday is a delight instead of a bore to a man with a hobby. Thrown out of his usual occupations on a holiday, the average man is at a loss for employment. Provided his neighbors are in the same fix, he can play cards. But there are hobbies and hobbies. As an occasional relaxation, for example, nothing can be said against card-playing. But as a hobby it is not much better than " collecting strings." It is neither broadening mentally nor invigorating physically, and it closes the door upon other interests which are both. I remember that once, on a long sea-voyage, I envied certain of my fellow-passengers who found amusement in cards when the conditions were such as to make almost any other occupation out of the question. But when finally the ship's course lay along a strange coast, winding among unfamiliar islands, by shores luxuriant with tropical vegetation and sprinkled with strange settlements, all affording delight to the eye and interest to the mind, these players who had come abroad solely for instruction and pleasure could not be enticed from their tables, and I thanked my stars that I had not fallen under the stultifying sway of cards. Much the same gratitude is aroused when I see men and women spending precious summer days indoors over the card-table when they might be breathing the fragrant, life-giving air, and rejoicing in the beauty and interest of the woods and fields.

All things considered, a hobby that takes us out of doors is the best. The different open-air sports may be classed under this head. The chief lack in the artificial sports, such as polo, golf, baseball, etc., as opposed to the natural sports, hunting and fishing, is that while they are invaluable as a means of health and relaxation, they do not lead to other and broader interests, while many a boy-hunter has developed into a naturalist as a result of long days in the woods. Hunting and fishing would seem almost perfect recreations were it not for the life-taking element, which may become brutalizing. I wish that every mother who believes in the value of natural sport for her young boys would set her face sternly against any taking of life that cannot be justified on the ground of man's needs, either in the way of protection or support.

The ideal hobby, it seems to me, is one that keeps us in the open air among inspiring surroundings, with the knowledge of natural objects as the end in view. The study of plants, of animals, of the earth itself, botany, zoölogy, or geology, any one of these will answer the varied requirements of an ideal hobby. Potentially they possess all the elements of sport. Often they require not only perseverance and skill but courage and daring. They are a means of health, a relaxation to the mind from ordinary cares, and an absorbing interest. Any one of them may be used as a doorway to the others.

If parents realized the value to their childrens' minds and bodies of a love for plants and animals, of any such hobby as birds or butterflies or trees or flowers, I am sure they would take more pains to encourage the interest which instinctively a child feels in these things. It must be because such realization is lacking that we see parents apparently either too indolent or too ignorant to share the enthusiasm and to satisfy the curiosity awakened in the child's active mind by natural objects.

Of course it is possible that owing to the strange reticence of many children, parents may be unconscious of the existence of any enthusiasm or curiosity of this sort. As a little child I was so eager to know the names of the wild flowers that I went through my grandfather's library, examining book after book on flowers in the vain hope of acquiring the desired information. Always after more or less tedious reading, for I was too young to master tables of contents and introductions, I would discover that the volume under examination was devoted to garden flowers. But I do not remember that it occurred to me to tell anyone what I wanted or to ask

3

for help. Finally I learned that a book on the subject, written "for young people," was in existence, and I asked my mother to buy it for me. The request was gratified promptly and I plodded through the preliminary matter of "How Plants Grow" to find that I was quite unable to master the key, and that any knowledge of the flowers that could appeal to my child-mind was locked away from me as hopelessly as before. Even though my one expressed wish had been so gladly met, I did not confide to others my perplexity, but surrendered sadly a cherished dream. Owing largely, I believe, to the reaction from this disappointment, it was many years before I attempted again to wrestle with a botanical key, or to learn the names of the flowers.

How much was lost by yielding too easily to discouragement I not only realize now, but I realized it partially during the long period when the plants were nameless. Among the flowers whose faces were familiar though their names were unknown, I felt that I was not making the most of my opportunities. And when I met plants which were both new and nameless, I was a stranger indeed. In the English woods and along the lovely English rivers, by the rushing torrents and in the Alpine meadows of Switzerland, on the mountains of Brazil, I should have felt myself less an alien had I been able then as now to detect the kinship between foreign and North American plants, and to call the strangers by names that were at least partially familiar.

To the man or woman who is somewhat at home

in the plant-world, travel is quite a different thing from what it is to one who does not know a mint from a mustard. The shortest journey to a new locality is full of interest to the traveller who is striving to lengthen his list of plant acquaintances. The tedious waits around the railway station are welcomed as opportunities for fresh discoveries. The slow local train receives blessings instead of anathemas because of the superiority of its windows as posts of observation. The long stage ride is too short to satisfy the plant-lover who is keeping count of the different species by the roadside.

While crossing the continent on the Canadian Pacific Railway a few years ago, the days spent in traversing the vast plains east of the Rockies were days of keen enjoyment on account of the new plants seen from my window and gathered breathlessly for identification during the brief stops. But to most of my fellow-passengers they were days of unmitigated boredom. They could not comprehend the reluctance with which I met each nightfall as an interruption to my watch.

When, finally, one cold June morning we climbed the glorious Canadian Rockies and were driven to the hotel at Banff, where we were to rest for twenty-four hours, the enjoyment of the previous week was crowned by seeing the dining-room tables decorated with a flower which I had never succeeded in finding in the woods at home. It was the lovely little orchid, *Calypso borealis*, a shy, wild creature which had been brought to me from the

5

mountains of Vermont. It seemed almost desecration to force this little aristocrat to consort with the pepper-pots and pickles of a hotel dining-room. In my eagerness to see Calypso in her forest-home I could scarcely wait to eat the breakfast for which a few moments before I had been painfully hungry.

Unfortunately the waiters at Banff were proved as ruthless as vandals in other parts of the world. Among the pines that clothed the lower mountainsides I found many plants of Calypso, but only one or two of the delicate blossoms had been left to gladden the eyes of those who love to see a flower in the wild beauty of its natural surroundings.

That same eventful day had in store for me another delight as the result of my love for plants. For a long time I had wished to know the shooting-star, a flower with whose general appearance from pictures or from descriptions I was familiar. I knew that it grew in this part of the world, but during a careful search of the woods and meadows and of the banks of the rushing streams the only shooting-star I discovered was a faded blossom which someone had picked and flung upon the mountain-path. Late in the afternoon, having given up the hope of any fresh find, I went for a swim in the warm sulphur pool. While paddling about the clear water, revelling in the beauty of the surroundings and the sheer physical joy of the moment, my eyes fell suddenly on a cluster of pink, cyclamen-like blossoms springing from the opposite rocks. I recognized at once the pretty shooting-star.

Two days later, at Glacier, I had another pleasure from the same source in the discovery of great beds of nodding golden lilies, the western species of adder's tongue, growing close to white fields of snow.

"Ten thousand saw I at a glance,
Tossing their heads in sprightly dance."

The enjoyment of the entire trip to the Pacific coast, of the voyage among the islands and glaciers of Alaska, and of the journey home through the Yellowstone and across our Western prairies, was increased indescribably by the new plants I learned to know.

The pleasure we take in literature, as in travel, is enhanced by a knowledge of nature. Not only are we able better to appreciate writers on nature so original and inspiring as Thoreau, or so charming as John Burroughs, but such nature-loving poets as Wordsworth, Lowell, Bryant, and countless others, mean infinitely more to the man or woman who with a love of poetry combines a knowledge of the plants and birds mentioned in the poems.

Books of travel are usually far more interesting if we have some knowledge of botany and zoölogy. This is also true of biographies which deal with men or women who find either their work or their recreation—and how many men and women who have been powers for good may be counted in one class or the other—in some department of natural science.

One fascinating department of nature-study, that

7

of ferns, has received but little attention in this country. Within the last few years we have been supplied with excellent and inexpensive hand-books to our birds, butterflies, trees, and flowers. But so far as I know, with the exception of Mr. Williamson's little volume on the "Ferns of Kentucky," we have no book with sufficient text and illustrations within the reach of the brains and purse of the average fern-lover. In England one finds books of all sizes and prices on the English ferns, while our beautiful American ferns are almost unknown, owing probably to the lack of attractive and inexpensive fern literature. Eaton's finely illustrated work on the "Ferns of North America" is entirely out of the question on account of its expense; and the "Illustrated Flora" of Britton & Brown is also beyond the reach of the ordinary plant-lover. Miss Price's "Fern Collectors' Hand-book" is helpful, but it is without descriptive text. "Our Native Ferns and their Allies," by Mr. Underwood, is exhaustive and authoritative, but it is extremely technical and the different species are not illustrated. Mr. Dodge's pamphlet on the "Ferns and Fern Allies of New England" is excellent so far as it goes, the descriptions not being so technical as to confuse the beginner. But this also is not illustrated, while Mr. Knobel's pamphlet, "The Ferns and Evergreens of New England," has clear black-and-white illustrations of many species, but it has no text of importance.

In view of the singular grace and charm of the fern

8

tribe, patent to the most careless observer, this lack of fern literature is surprising. It is possible that Thoreau is right in claiming that " we all feel the ferns to be farther from us essentially and sympathetically than the phenogamous plants, the roses and weeds for instance." This may be true in spite of the fact that to some of us the charm of ferns is as great, their beauty more subtle, than that of the flowering plants, and to learn to know them by name, to trace them to their homes, and to observe their habits is attended with an interest as keen, perhaps keener, than that which attends the study of the names, haunts, and habits of the flowers.

That ferns possess a peculiar power of blinding their votaries to the actual position they occupy in the minds of people in general seems to me evidenced by the following quotations, taken respectively from Mr. Underwood's and Mr. Williamson's introductions.

So competent and coldly scientific an authority as Mr. Underwood opens his book with these words :

" In the entire vegetable world there are probably no forms of growth that attract more general notice than the Ferns."

The lack of fern literature, it seems to me, proves the fallacy of this statement. If ferns had been more generally noticed than other " forms of growth " in the vegetable world, surely more would have been written on the subject, and occasionally someone besides a botanist would be found who could name correctly more than three or four of our common wayside ferns.

In his introduction to the "Ferns of Kentucky," Mr. Williamson asks: "Who would now think of going to the country to spend a few days, or even one day, without first inquiring whether ferns are to be found in the locality?"

Though for some years I have been interested in ferns and have made many all-day country expeditions with various friends, I do not remember ever to have heard this question asked. Yet that two such writers as Mr. Underwood and Mr. Williamson could imagine the existence of a state of things so contrary to fact, goes far to prove the fascination of the study.

To the practical mind one of the great advantages of ferns as a hobby lies in the fact that the number of our native, that is, of our northeastern, ferns is so comparatively small as to make it an easy matter to learn to know by name and to see in their homes perhaps two-thirds of them.

On an ordinary walk of an hour or two through the fields and woods, the would-be fern student can familiarize himself with anywhere from ten to fifteen of the ferns described in this book. During a summer holiday in an average locality he should learn to know by sight and by name from twenty-five to thirty ferns, while in a really good neighborhood the enthusiast who is willing to scour the surrounding country from the tops of the highest mountains to the depths of the wildest ravines may hope to extend his list into the forties.

During the past year several lists of the ferns found on a single walk or within a certain radius have been published in the *Fern Bulletin*, leading to some rivalry between fern students who claim precedence for their pet localities.

Mr. Underwood has found twenty-seven species within the immediate vicinity of Green Lake, Onondaga County, N. Y., and thirty-four species within a circle whose diameter is not over three miles.

Mrs. E. H. Terry, on a two-hours' walk near Dorset, Vt., did still better. She found thirty-three species and four varieties, while Miss Margaret Slosson has broken the record by finding thirty-nine species and eight varieties, near Pittsford, Rutland County, Vt., within a triangle formed by "the end of a tamarack swamp, a field less than a mile away, and some limestone cliffs three miles from both the field and the end of the swamp."

Apart from the interest of extending one's list of fern acquaintances is that of discovering new stations for the rarer species. It was my good fortune last summer to make one of a party which found a previously unknown station for the rare Hart's Tongue, and I felt the thrill of excitement which attends such an experience. The other day, in looking over Torrey's "Flora of New York," I noticed the absence of several ferns now known to be natives of this State. When the fern student realizes the possibility which is always before him of finding a new station for a rare fern, and thus adding an item of value to the natural history of the State, he should be stimulated to fresh zeal.

Other interesting possibilities are those of discovering a new variety and of chancing upon those forked or crested fronds which appear occasionally in many species. These unusual forms not only possess the charm of rarity and sometimes of intrinsic beauty, but they are interesting because of the light it is believed they may throw on problems of fern ancestry. To this department of fern study, the discovery and development of abnormal forms, much attention is paid in England. In Lowe's "British Ferns" I find described between thirty and forty varieties of *Polypodium vulgare*, while the varieties of *Scolopendrium vulgare*, our rare Hart's Tongue, extend into the hundreds.

The majority of ferns mature late in the summer, giving the student the advantage of several weeks or months in which to observe their growth. Many of our most interesting flowers bloom and perish before we realize that the spring is really over. There are few flower lovers who have not had the sense of being outwitted by the rush of the season. Every year I make appointments with the different plants to visit them at their flowering time, and nearly every year I miss some such appointments through failure to appreciate the short lives of these fragile blossoms.

A few of the ferns share the early habits common to so many flowers. But usually we can hope to find them in their prime when most of the flowers have disappeared.

To me the greatest charm the ferns possess is that of their surroundings. No other plants know so well how to choose their haunts. If you wish to know the ferns you must follow them to Nature's most sacred retreats. In remote, tangled swamps, overhanging the swift, noiseless brook in the heart of the forest, close to the rush of the foaming waterfall, in the depths of some dark ravine, or perhaps high up on mountain-ledges, where the air is purer and the world wider and life more beautiful than we had fancied, these wild, graceful things are most at home.

You will never learn to know the ferns if you expect to make their acquaintance from a carriage, along the highway, or in the interval between two meals. For their sakes you must renounce indolent habits. You must be willing to tramp tirelessly through woods and across fields, to climb mountains and to scramble down gorges. You must be content with what luncheon you can carry in your pocket. And let me tell you this. When at last you fling yourself upon some bed of springing moss, and add to your sandwich cresses fresh and dripping from the neighboring brook, you will eat your simple meal with a relish that never attends the most elaborate luncheon within four walls. And when later you surrender yourself to the delicious sense of fatigue and drowsy relaxation which steals over you, mind and body, listening half-unconsciously to the plaintive, long-drawn notes of the wood-birds and the sharp "tsing" of the locusts, breathing the mingled fragrance of the mint at your feet and the pines and hemlocks overhead, you will wonder vaguely why on summer days you ever drive along the dusty high-road or eat indoors or do any of the flavorless conventional things that consume so large a portion of our lives.

Of course what is true of other out-door studies is true of the study of ferns. Constantly your curiosity is aroused by some bird-note, some tree, some gorgeously colored butterfly, and, in the case of ferns especially, by some outcropping rock, which make you eager to follow up other branches of nature-study, and to know by name each tree and bird and butterfly and rock you meet.

The immediate result of these long happy days is that "golden doze of mind which follows upon much exercise in the open air," the "ecstatic stupor" which Stevenson supposes to be the nearly chronic condition of "open-air laborers." Surely there is no such preventive of insomnia, no such cure for nervousness or morbid introspection as an absorbing out-door interest. Body and mind alike are invigorated to a degree that cannot be appreciated by one who has not experienced the life-giving power of some such close and loving contact with nature.

# WHEN AND WHERE TO FIND FERNS

" It is no use to direct our steps to the woods if they do not carry us thither. I am alarmed when it happens that I have walked a mile into the woods bodily, without getting there in spirit."— *Thoreau*

# WHEN AND WHERE TO FIND FERNS

It is in early spring that one likes to take up for the first time an out-door study. But if you begin your search for ferns in March, when the woods are yielding a few timid blossoms, and the air, still pungent with a suggestion of winter, vibrates to the lisping notes of newly arrived birds, you will hardly be rewarded by finding any but the evergreen species, and even these are not likely to be especially conspicuous at this season.

Usually it is the latter part of April before the pioneers among the ferns, the great Osmundas, push up the big, woolly croziers, or fiddleheads, which will soon develop into the most luxuriant and tropical-looking plants of our low wet woods and roadsides.

At about the same time, down among last year's Christmas Ferns, you find the rolled-up fronds of this year, covered with brown or whitish scales. And now every day for many weeks will appear fresh batches of young ferns. Someone has said that there is nothing more aggressively new-born than a young fern, and this thought will recur constantly as you chance upon the little wrinkled crozier-like fronds, whether they are bundled up in wrappings of soft wool or protected by a garment of overlapping scales, or whether, like many of the later arrivals, they come into the world as naked and puny as a human baby.

Once uncurled, the ferns lose quickly this look of infancy, and embody, quite as effectively, even the hardiest and coarsest among them, the slender grace of youth. Early in May we find the Osmundas in this stage of their development. The Royal Fern, smooth and delicate, is now flushing the wet meadows with its tender red. In the open woods and along the roadside the Interrupted and the Cinnamon Ferns wear a green equally delicate. These three plants soon reach maturity and are conspicuous by reason of their unusual size and their flower-like fruit-clusters.

On the rocky banks of the brook, or perhaps among the spreading roots of some forest-tree, the Fragile Bladder Fern unrolls its tremulous little

Fiddleheads

fronds, on which the fruit-dots soon appear. Where there is less moisture and more exposure we may find the Rusty Woodsia, now belying its name by its silvery aspect. At this same season in the bogs and thickets we should look for the curious little Adder's Tongue.

By the first of June many of the ferns are well advanced. On the hill-sides and along the wood-path the Brake spreads its single umbrella-like frond, now pale green and delicate, quite unlike the umbrageous-looking plant of a month later. Withdrawing into the recesses formed by the pasture-rails the Lady Fern is in its first freshness, without any sign of the disfigurements it develops so often by the close of the summer. Great patches of yellowish green in the wet meadows draw attention to the Sensitive Fern, which only at this season seems to have any claim to its

Fragile Bladder Fern

title. The Virginia Chain Fern is another plant to be looked for in the wet June meadows. It is one of the few ferns which grows occasionally in deep water.

The Maidenhair, though immature, is lovely in its fragility. Thoreau met with it on June 13th and

Crested
Shield Fern

describes
it in his
diary for
that day: "The
delicate maiden-hair fern
forms a cup or dish,
very delicate and graceful. Beautiful, too, its
glossy black stem and
its wave-edged, fruited
leaflets."

In the crevices of lofty cliffs the Mountain
Spleenwort approaches
maturity. And now we
should search the moist,
mossy crannies of the
rocks for the Slender Cliff
Brake, for in some localities
this plant disappears early in
the summer.

We may hope to find most of
the ferns in full foliage, if not in
fruit, by the middle of July. Dark
green, tall and vigorous stand the
Brakes. The Crested Shield Fern is
fruiting in the swamps, and in the deeper woods Clinton's and Goldie's Ferns
are in full fruitage. Magnificent vase-like clusters of the Ostrich Fern spread above our

heads in the thicket along the river-shore. The
Spinulose Shield Fern and the Evergreen Wood
Fern meet us at every turn of the shaded path
beside the brook, and on the rocky wooded hill-
side the Christmas Fern is almost as abundant.
Where the stream plunges from above, the Bulblet Bladder Fern drapes the steep banks with its
long feathery fronds. In the wet meadows and
thickets the New York Fern and the Marsh
Shield Fern are noticeable on account of their
light green color and delicate texture. On mountain-ledges we look for the little Woodsias, and in
rocky places, often in the shadow of red cedars, for
the slim erect fronds of the Ebony Spleenwort.

Possibly it will be our good fortune to discover
the blue-green foliage of the Purple Cliff Brake
springing from the crevices of some dry limestone
cliff. Almost surely, if we search the moist, shaded
rocks and ravines in the neighborhood, we shall
greet with unfailing pleasure the lovely little
Maidenhair Spleenwort.

In somewhat southern localities the tapering,
yellow-green fronds of the *Dicksonia* or Hay-scented Fern are even more abundant and conspicuous
than the darker foliage of the Spinulose Shield Fern.
They abound along the roadsides and in partially
shaded or open pastures, the spores ripening not
earlier than August.

In the same month we find in full maturity three
interesting wood ferns, all belonging to the same
group. The first of these is the Long Beech Fern.

It is abundant in many of our northern woods and on the rocky banks of streams. Its shape is noticeably triangular, the triangle being longer than broad. Its texture is rather soft and downy. The lowest pair of pinnæ stand forward and are conspicuously deflexed, giving an easy clew to the plant's identity.

The most attractive member of the group to my mind is the Oak Fern. I find it growing abundantly in the cedar swamps and wet woods of somewhat northern localities. Its delicate, spreading,

Purple Cliff
Brake

three-branched frond suggests that of a young Brake. This plant is peculiarly dainty in the early summer, as frequently later in the year it becomes blotched and disfigured.

The Broad Beech Fern seeks drier neighborhoods, and often a more southern locality than its two kinsmen. Its triangular fronds, broader than they are long, are conspicuous on account of the unusual size of the lowest pair of pinnæ.

A common plant in the rich August woods is the Virginia Grape Fern, with its spreading leaf and branching fruit-cluster. The rather coarsely cut fronds of the Silvery Spleenwort are also frequently met with in the same neighborhood. Occasionally in their companionship we find the delicate and attractive Narrow-leaved Spleenwort.

August is the month that should be chosen for expeditions in search of some of our rarest ferns. In certain wild ravines of Central New York, at the foot of shaded limestone cliffs, the glossy leaves of the Hart's Tongue are actually weighed down by the brown, velvety rows of sporangia which emboss their lower surfaces. Over the rocks near-by, the quaint, though less unusual, Walking Leaf runs riot. Perhaps in the crevices of the overhanging cliff the little Rue Spleenwort has secured a foothold for its tiny fronds, their backs nearly covered with confluent fruit-dots.

On the mountain-ledges of Northern New England we should look for the Green Spleenwort, and for the Fragrant Shield Fern. Along rocky mountain-streams Braun's Holly Fern may be found. In wet woods, usually near the coast, the Net-veined Chain Fern is occasionally conspicuous.

More southern localities must be visited if we wish to see in its home the Hairy Lip Fern, whose most northern stations were on the Hudson River (for I do not know if this plant can be found there at

present), and such rare
Spleenworts as the Pin-
natifid, Scott's and Bradley's.

In September the
fruit-clusters of the little Curly Grass ripen
in the low pine barrens
of New Jersey. Over
moist thickets, in rarely
favored retreats from
Massachusetts south-
ward, clamber the
slender strands of
the Climbing Fern.

Thoreau's di-
ary of Sep-
tember 26th
evidently re-
fers to this
plant: " The
tree-fern is in

Ternate Grape Fern

fruit now, with its delicate, tendril-like fruit, climbing three or four feet over the asters, golden-rod, etc., on the edge of the swamp."

In moist places now we find the triangular much dissected leaf and branching fruit-cluster of the Ternate Grape Fern.

When October sets in, many of the ferns take their color-note from the surroundings. Vying with the maples along the roadside the Osmundas wear deep orange. Many of the fronds of the *Dicksonia* are bleached almost white, while others look fresh and green despite their delicate texture. On October 4th Thoreau writes of this plant:

" How interesting now, by wall-sides and on open springy hill-sides, the large straggling tufts of the Dicksonia fern above the leaf-strewn green sward, the cold, fall-green sward! They are unusually preserved about the Corner Spring, considering the earliness of this year. Long, handsome, lanceolate green fronds pointing in every direction, recurved and full of fruit, intermixed with yellowish and sere brown and shrivelled ones, the whole clump perchance strewn with fallen and withered maple leaves, and overtopped by now withered and unnoticed osmundas. Their lingering greenness is so much the more noticeable now that the leaves generally have changed. They affect us as if they were evergreen, such persistent life and greenness in the midst of decay. No matter how much they are strewn with withered leaves, moist and green they spire above them, not fearing the frosts, fragile as they are.

25

Their greenness is so much the more interesting, because so many have already fallen, and we know that the first severe frost will cut off them too. In the summer greenness is cheap, now it is a thing comparatively rare, and is the emblem of life to us."

Oddly enough, with the first approach of winter the vigorous-looking Brake turns brown and quickly withers, usually without passing through any intermediate gradations of yellow.

In November we notice chiefly the evergreen ferns. The great round fruit-dots of the Polypody show distinctly through the fronds as they stand erect in the sunlight. A sober green, looking as though it were warranted fast, is the winter dress of the Evergreen Wood Fern. The Christmas Fern, bright and glossy, reminds one that the holiday season is not distant. These three plants are especially conspicuous in our late autumn woods. Their brave and cheerful endurance is always a delight. Later in the season the curled pinnæ of the Polypody seem to be making the best of cold weather. The fronds of the Christmas Fern and the Evergreen Wood Fern, still fresh and green, lie prostrate on the ground, their weakened stems apparently unable to support them erect, but undoubtedly in this position they are the better protected from the storm and stress of winter.

Many other ferns are more or less evergreen, but perhaps none are so important to our fall rambles as this sturdy group. Several of the Rock Spleenworts are evergreen, but their ordinarily diminutive stature dwindles with the increasing cold, and we seldom encounter them on our winter walks. The sterile fronds of a number of the Shield Ferns endure till spring. The Purple Cliff Brake and the Walking Leaf are also proof against ice and snow. Even in the middle of January the keen-eyed fern hunter may hope to make some discovery of interest regarding the haunts and habits of his favorites.

Evergreen Wood Fern

# EXPLANATION OF TERMS

A FERN is a flowerless plant growing from a *rootstock* (*a*), with leaves or *fronds* usually raised on a stalk, rolled up (*b*) in the bud,* and bearing on their lower surfaces (*c*) the *spores*, by means of which the plant reproduces.

A *rootstock* is an underground, rooting stem. Ferns are propagated by the growth and budding of the rootstock as well as by the ordinary method of reproduction. The fronds spring from the rootstock in the manner peculiar to the species to which they belong. The Osmundas, the Evergreen Wood Fern, and others grow in a crown or circle, the younger fronds always inside. The Mountain Spleenwort is one of a class which has irregularly clus-

* *Ophioglossum* and the Botrychiums, not being true ferns, are exceptions.

Polypody

28

tered fronds. The fronds of the Brake are more or less solitary, rising from distinct and somewhat distant portions of the rootstock. The Botrychiums usually give birth to a single frond each season, the base of the stalk containing the bud for the succeeding year.

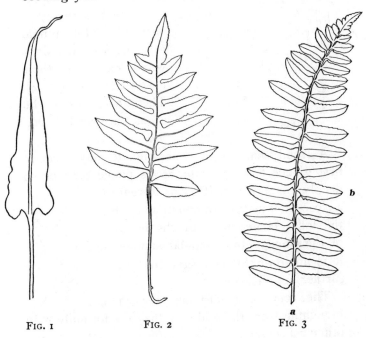

FIG. 1          FIG. 2                    FIG. 3

A frond is *simple* when it consists of an undivided leaf such as that of the Hart's Tongue or of the Walking Leaf (Fig. 1).

A frond is *pinnatifid* when cut so as to form lobes extending half-way or more to the midvein (Fig. 2).

29

A frond is *once-pinnate* when the incisions extend to the midvein (Fig. 3).

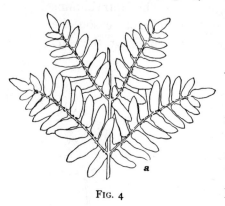

FIG. 4

Under these conditions the midvein is called the *rachis* (*a*), and the divisions are called the *pinnæ* (*b*).

A frond is *twice-pinnate* when the pinnæ are cut into divisions which extend to their midveins (Fig. 4). These divisions of the pinnæ are called *pinnules* (*a*).

A frond that is only once-pinnate may seem at first glance twice-pinnate, as its pinnæ may be so deeply lobed or pinnatifid as to require a close examination to convince us that the lobes come short of the midvein of the pinnæ. In a popular hand-book it is not thought necessary to explain further modifications.

FIG. 5

The veins of a fern are *free* when, branching from the midvein, they do not unite with other veins (Fig. 5).

FIG. 6

Ferns produce *spores* (Fig. 6) instead of seeds. These spores are collected in spore-cases or *sporangia* (Fig. 7). Usually the sporangia are clustered in dots or lines on the back of a frond or along its margins. These patches of sporangia are called *sori* or *fruit-*

*dots.* They take various shapes in the different species. They may be round or linear or oblong or kidney-shaped or curved. At times they are naked, but more frequently they are covered by a minute outgrowth of the frond or by its reflexed margin. This covering is called the *indusium.* In systematic botanies the indusia play an important part in determining genera. But as often they are so minute as to be almost invisible to the naked eye, and, as frequently they wither away early

FIG. 7

in the season, I place little dependence upon them as a means of popular identification.

A *fertile* frond is one which bears spores.

A *sterile* frond is one without spores.

# FERTILIZATION, DEVELOPMENT, AND FRUCTIFICATION OF FERNS

UNTIL very recently the development of ferns, their methods of fertilization and fructification have been shrouded in mystery. At one period it was believed that "fern-seed," as the fern-spores were called, possessed various miraculous powers. These were touched upon frequently by the early poets. In Shakespeare's "Henry IV" Gadshill exclaims:

"We have the receipt of fern-seed, we walk invisible."

He is met with the rejoinder:

"Nay, I think rather you are more beholden to the night than to fern-seed, for your walking invisible."

One of Ben Jonson's characters expresses the same idea in much the same words:

"I had no medicine, sir, to walk invisible,
No fern-seed in my pocket."

In Butler's "Hudibras" reference is made to the anxieties we needlessly create for ourselves:

"That spring like fern, that infant weed,
Equivocally without seed,
And have no possible foundation
But merely in th' imagination."

32

In view of the fact that many ferns bear their spores or "fern-seed" somewhat conspicuously on the lower surfaces of their fronds, it seems probable that the "fern" of early writers was our common Brake, the fructification of which is more than usually obscure, its sporangia or "fern-seed" being concealed till full maturity by the reflexed margin of its frond. This plant is, perhaps, the most abundant and conspicuous of English ferns. Miss Pratt believes it to be the "fearn" of the Anglo-Saxons, and says that to its profusion in their neighborhood many towns and hamlets, such as Fearnborough or Farnborough, Farningham, Farnhow, and others owe their titles. The plant is a noticeable and common one also on the Continent.

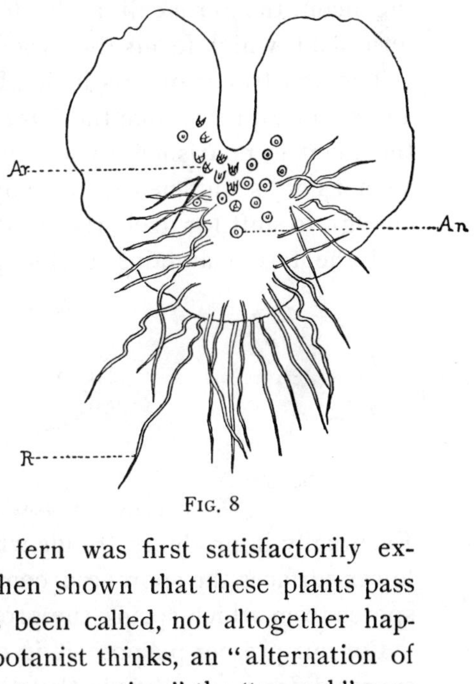

FIG. 8

In 1848 the development of the fern was first satisfactorily explained. It was then shown that these plants pass through what has been called, not altogether happily the modern botanist thinks, an "alternation of generations." One "generation," the "sexual," consists of a tiny, green, plate-like object, termed the

33

*prothallium* (Fig. 8). This is connected with the soil by hair-like roots. On its lower surface are borne usually both the reproductive organs of the fern, the *antheridia*, corresponding to the stamens or fertilizing organs of the flower, and the *archegonia*, performing the office of the flower's pistils, inasmuch as their germ-cells receive the fertilizing substance produced by the *antheridia*. But no seeds are formed as the result of this fertilization. Instead of this seed-formation which we note in the flowering plant, the germ-cell in the fern develops into a fern-plant, which forms the "asexual" generation.

The first fronds of this little plant are very small and simple, quite unlike the later ones. For a time the plant is nourished by the prothallium, but as soon as it is sufficiently developed and vigorous enough to shift for itself, the prothallium dies away, and the fern maintains an independent existence.

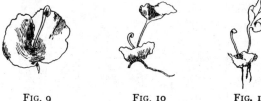

FIG. 9        FIG. 10        FIG. 11

First fronds of Maidenhair

Eventually it produces fronds which bear on their lower surfaces the sporangia containing the minute spores from which spring the prothallia.

For our present purpose it is enough to say that spores differ from seeds in that they are not the immediate result of the interaction of reproductive

34

organs. They resemble seeds in that they are expelled from the parent-plant on attaining maturity, and germinate on contact with the moist earth.

Thus it is seen that the life-cycle of a fern consists of two stages:

First, the prothallium, bearing the reproductive organs; second, the fern-plant proper, developing the spores which produce the prothallium.

Along the moist, shaded banks of the wood road, or on decaying stumps, keen eyes will discern frequently the tiny green prothallia, although they are somewhat difficult to find except in the green-house where one can see them in abundance either in the boxes used for growing the young plants, or on the moist surfaces of flower-pots, where the spores have fallen accidentally and have germinated.

As the fertilization of the germ-cell in the archegonium cannot take place except under water, perhaps the fact is accounted for that ferns are found chiefly in moist places. This water may be only a sufficient amount of rain or dew to permit the antherozoids or fertilizing cells of the antheridium to swim to the archegonium, which they enter for the purpose of fertilizing the germ-cell.

It is interesting to examine with a good magnifying glass the sporangia borne on the lower surface of a mature fertile frond. In many species each sporangium or spore-case is surrounded with an elastic ring, which at maturity contracts so suddenly as to rupture the spore-case, and cause the expulsion of the numberless spores (Fig. 7).

# NOTABLE FERN FAMILIES

### OSMUNDA (Flowering Ferns)

Tall swamp ferns, growing in large crowns, with the fertile fronds or portions *conspicuously unlike* the sterile ; sporangia opening by a longitudinal cleft into two valves.

### ONOCLEA

Coarse ferns, with the fertile fronds rolled up into necklace-like or berry-like segments, and *entirely unlike* the broad, pinnatifid sterile ones. Fertile fronds unrolling at maturity, allowing the spores to escape, and remaining long after the sterile fronds have perished ; sporangia stalked, ringed, bursting transversely.

### WOODSIA

Small or medium-sized ferns, growing among rocks, with 1–2 pinnate or pinnatifid fronds and round fruit-dots ; indusium thin and often evanescent, attached by its base under the sporangia, either small and open, or else early bursting at the top into irregular pieces or lobes ; sporangia stalked, ringed, bursting transversely.

### CYSTOPTERIS (Bladder Ferns)

Delicate rock or wood ferns, with 2–3 pinnate fronds and round fruit-dots ; indusium hood-like, attached by a broad base to the inner side, soon thrown back or withering away ; sporangia as above.

### ASPIDIUM (Shield Ferns)

Ferns with 1–3 pinnate fronds and round fruit-dots ; indusium more or less flat, fixed by its depressed centre ; sporangia as above.

## PHEGOPTERIS (Beech Ferns)

Medium-sized or small ferns, with 2–3 pinnatifid or ternate leaves, and small, round, uncovered fruit-dots; sporangia as above.

## WOODWARDIA (Chain Ferns)

Large and rather coarse ferns of swamps or wet woods, fronds pinnate or nearly twice-pinnate; fruit-dots oblong or linear, sunk in cavities of the leaf and arranged in chain-like rows; indusium lid-like, somewhat leathery, fixed by its outer margin to a veinlet; veins more or less reticulated; sporangia as above.

## ASPLENIUM (Spleenworts)

Large or small ferns, with varying fronds and linear or oblong fruit-dots; indusium straight or curved; sporangia as above.

## PELLÆA (Cliff Brakes)

Small or medium-sized rock ferns, with pinnate fronds and sporangia borne beneath the reflexed margins of the pinnæ; sporangia as above.

## BOTRYCHIUM (Moonworts)

*(Belonging to the Fern Allies)*

Fleshy plants, with fronds (usually solitary) divided into a sterile and a fertile portion, the bud for the succeeding year embedded in the base of the stem.

# HOW TO USE THE BOOK

BEFORE attempting to identify the ferns by means of the following Guide it would be well to turn to the Explanation of Terms, and with as many species as you can conveniently collect, on the table before you, to master the few necessary technical terms, that you may be able to distinguish a frond that is pinnatifid from one that is pinnate, a pinna from a pinnule, a fertile from a sterile frond.

You should bear in mind that in some species the fertile fronds are so unleaf-like in appearance that to the uninitiated they do not suggest fronds at all. The fertile fronds of the Onocleas, for example, are so contracted as to conceal any resemblance to the sterile ones. They appear to be mere clusters of fruit. The fertile fronds of the Cinnamon Fern are equally unleaf-like, as are the fertile portions of the other Osmundas and of several other species.

In your rambles through the fields and woods your eyes will soon learn to detect hitherto unnoticed species. In gathering specimens you will take heed to break off the fern as near the ground as possible, and you will not be satisfied till you have secured both a fertile and a sterile frond. In carrying them home you will remember the necessity of keeping together the fronds which belong to the same plant.

When sorting your finds you will group them according to the Guide. The broad-leaved Sensitive Fern, with its separate, dark-green fruit cluster, makes its way necessarily to Group I. To Group II goes your pale-fronded Royal Fern, tipped with brown sporangia. As a matter of course you lay in Group III the leaf-like but dissimilar sterile and fertile fronds of the Slender Cliff Brake. The spreading Brake, its reflexed margin covering the sporangia, identifies itself with Group IV. The oblong fruit-dots of the little Mountain Spleenwort carry it to Group V, while the round ones, like pinheads, of the Evergreen Wood Fern announce it a member of Group VI.

The different ferns sorted, it will be a simple matter to run quickly through the brief descriptions under the different Groups till you are referred to the descriptions in the body of the book of the species under investigation.

# GUIDE

FOR the purpose of identification the ferns described are arranged in six groups, according to their manner of fruiting.

## GROUP I

### STERILE AND FERTILE FRONDS TOTALLY UNLIKE; FERTILE FRONDS NOT LEAF-LIKE IN APPEARANCE

#### 1. SENSITIVE FERN

*Onoclea sensibilis*

Sterile fronds usually large; broadly triangular, deeply pinnatifid. Fertile fronds much contracted, with berry-like pinnules. In wet meadows. P. 54.

#### 2. OSTRICH FERN

*Onoclea Struthiopteris*

Large. Sterile fronds once-pinnate, pinnæ pinnatifid. Fertile fronds contracted, with necklace-like pinnæ. Along streams and in moist woods. P. 56.

#### 3. CINNAMON FERN

*Osmunda cinnamomea*

Large. Sterile fronds once-pinnate, pinnæ pinnatifid. Fertile fronds composed of cinnamon-brown fruit-clusters. In wet places. P. 60.

#### 4. CURLY GRASS

*Schizæa pusilla*

Very small. Sterile fronds linear, grass-like. Fertile fronds taller, with a terminal fruit-cluster. In pine barrens of New Jersey. P. 63.

# GROUP II

## FERTILE FRONDS PARTIALLY LEAF-LIKE, THE FERTILE PORTION UNLIKE THE REST OF THE FROND

[The species coming under the genera *Botrychium* and *Ophioglossum* may appear to belong to Group I, as the fertile and the sterile portions of their fronds may seem to the uninitiated like separate fronds, but in reality they belong to the one frond.]

### 5. ROYAL FERN

*Osmunda regalis*

Large. Sterile fronds twice-pinnate, pinnules oblong. Fertile fronds leaf-like below, sporangia in clusters at their summits. In wet places. P. 67.

### 6. INTERRUPTED FERN

*Osmunda Claytoniana*

Large. Sterile fronds once-pinnate, pinnæ pinnatifid. Fertile fronds leaf-like above and below, contracted in the middle with brown fruit-clusters. In wet places. P. 72.

### 7. CLIMBING FERN

*Lygodium palmatum*

Climbing, with lobed, palmate pinnæ and terminal fruit-clusters. Moist thickets and open woods. Rare. P. 75.

### 8. ADDER'S TONGUE

*Ophioglossum vulgatum*

Small. Sterile portion an ovate leaf. Fertile portion a slender spike. In moist meadows. P. 77.

### 9. RATTLESNAKE FERN

*Botrychium Virginianum*

Rather large. Sterile portion a thin, spreading, ternately divided leaf with three primary divisions; 1–2 pinnate. Fertile portion a branching fruit-cluster. In rich woods. P. 80.

41

### 10. TERNATE GRAPE FERN

*Botrychium ternatum* or *dissectum*

Of varying size, very fleshy. Sterile portion a broadly triangular, ternate, finely dissected leaf, long-stalked from near the base of the stem. Fertile portion a branching fruit-cluster. In moist meadows. P. 81.

### 11. LITTLE GRAPE FERN

*Botrychium simplex*

A very small fleshy plant. Sterile portion an oblong leaf more or less lobed. Fertile portion a simple or slightly branching spike. In moist woods and in fields. P. 82.

### 12. MOONWORT

*Botrychium Lunaria*

Usually small, very fleshy. Sterile portion divided into several fan-shaped lobes. Fertile portion a branching fruit-cluster. Mostly in fields. P. 84.

### 13. MATRICARY GRAPE FERN

*Botrychium matricariæfolium*

Small, more or less fleshy. Sterile portion ovate or oblong, once or twice pinnatifid. Fertile portion a branching fruit-cluster. In grassy woods and wet meadows. P. 86.

### 14. LANCE-LEAVED GRAPE FERN

*Botrychium lanceolatum*

Small, scarcely fleshy. Sterile portion triangular, twice-pinnatifid. Fertile portion a branching fruit-cluster. In woods and meadows. P. 86.

# GROUP III

### FERTILE FRONDS UNIFORMLY SOMEWHAT LEAF-LIKE IN APPEARANCE, YET DIFFERING NOTICEABLY FROM STERILE FRONDS

## 15. SLENDER CLIFF BRAKE

*Pellæa gracilis*

A small fern, 1–3 pinnate. Very delicate. Fertile fronds taller, more contracted and simpler than the sterile, sporangia bordering the pinnæ. Usually on sheltered rocks, preferring limestone. P. 87.

## 16. PURPLE CLIFF BRAKE

*Pellæa atropurpurea*

Medium sized, 1–2 pinnate, leathery. Fertile fronds taller and more contracted than the sterile, sporangia bordering the pinnæ. Usually on exposed rocks, preferring limestone. P. 90.

## 17. CHRISTMAS FERN

*Aspidium acrostichoides*

Rather large, smooth and glossy, once-pinnate. Fertile fronds contracted at the summit where the fruit appears. In rocky woods. P. 96.

## 18. NARROW-LEAVED SPLEENWORT

*Asplenium angustifolium*

Tall and delicate, once-pinnate. Fertile fronds taller and narrower than the sterile. In moist woods in late summer. P. 98.

## 19. NET-VEINED CHAIN FERN

*Woodwardia angustifolia*

Large, fronds deeply pinnatifid, the fertile taller and more contracted than the sterile. In wet woods near the coast. P. 102.

# GROUP IV

FERTILE AND STERILE FRONDS LEAF-LIKE AND SIMILAR;
SPORANGIA ON OR BENEATH A REFLEXED PORTION
OF THE MARGIN

[The first clause bars out *P. gracilis* and *P. atropurpurea*, which otherwise would belong to Group IV as well as to Group III.]

## 20. BRAKE

*Pteris aquilina*

Large and coarse, frond 3-branched, spreading, each branch 2-pinnate, sporangia in a continuous line beneath the reflexed margin of the frond. In dry, somewhat open places. P. 105.

## 21. MAIDENHAIR

*Adiantum pedatum*

Graceful and delicate, frond forked at the summit of the stem, 2-pinnate, the pinnæ springing from the upper sides of the branches, pinnules one-sided, their upper margins lobed, bearing on their undersides the short fruit-dots. In rich woods. P. 108.

## 22. HAIRY LIP FERN

*Cheilanthes vestita*

Rather small, fronds 2-pinnate, hairy, fruit-dots "covered by the infolded ends of the rounded or oblong lobes." On rocks. P. 112.

## 23. HAY-SCENTED FERN

*Dicksonia pilosiuscula*

Rather large, pale, delicate and sweet-scented, fronds usually 2-pinnate, fruit-dots small, each on a recurved toothlet of the pinnule, borne on an elevated, globular receptacle. In moist thickets and in upland pastures. P. 114.

44

# GROUP V

FERTILE AND STERILE FRONDS LEAF-LIKE AND SIMILAR;
SPORANGIA IN LINEAR OR OBLONG FRUIT-DOTS

### 24. LADY FERN

*Asplenium Filix-fœmina*

Rather large, fronds 2-pinnate, fruit-dots curved, often horse-shoe shaped, finally confluent. In moist woods and along roadsides. P. 120.

### 25. SILVERY SPLEENWORT

*Asplenium thelypteroides*

Large, fronds once-pinnate, pinnæ deeply pinnatifid, lobes oblong and obtuse, fruit-dots oblong, silvery when young. In rich woods. P. 124.

### 26. RUE SPLEENWORT

*Asplenium Ruta-muraria*

Very small, fronds loosely 2–3 pinnate at base, pinnatifid above, fruit-dots linear-oblong, confluent when mature. On limestone cliffs. Rare. P. 126.

### 27. MOUNTAIN SPLEENWORT

*Asplenium montanum*

Small, fronds 1–2 pinnate, fruit-dots linear-oblong, often confluent. On rocks. P. 130.

### 28. EBONY SPLEENWORT

*Asplenium ebeneum*

Fronds slender and erect, once-pinnate, pinnæ eared on the upper or on both sides, stalk and rachis blackish and shining, fruit-dots oblong. On rocks and hill-sides. P. 134.

45

## 29. MAIDENHAIR SPLEENWORT

*Asplenium Trichomanes*

Small, fronds once-pinnate, pinnæ roundish, stalk and rachis purplish-brown and shining, fruit-dots short.    In crevices of rocks. P. 136.

## 30. GREEN SPLEENWORT

*Asplenium viride*

Small, fronds linear, once-pinnate, brownish stalk passing into a green rachis.   On shaded cliffs northward.   P. 138.

## 31. SCOTT'S SPLEENWORT

*Asplenium ebenoides*

Small, fronds pinnate below, pinnatifid above, apex slender and prolonged, stalk and rachis blackish, fruit-dots straight or slightly curved.   On limestone.   Very rare.   P. 140.

## 32. PINNATIFID SPLEENWORT

*Asplenium pinnatifidum*

Small, fronds pinnatifid, or the lower part pinnate, tapering above into a slender prolongation, stalk blackish, passing into a green rachis, fruit-dots straight or slightly curved.   On rocks.   Rare. P. 142.

## 33. BRADLEY'S SPLEENWORT

*Asplenium Bradleyi*

Small, once-pinnate, pinnæ lobed or toothed, stalk and rachis chestnut-brown, fruit-dots short.   On rocks, preferring limestone. Very rare.   P. 144.

## 34. WALKING FERN

*Camptosorus rhizophyllus*

Small, fronds undivided, heart-shaped at the base or sometimes with prolonged basal ears, tapering above to a prolonged point which roots, forming a new plant, fruit-dots oblong or linear, irregularly scattered.   On shaded rocks, preferring limestone.   P. 146.

## 35. HART'S TONGUE

*Scolopendrium vulgare*

Fronds a few inches to nearly two feet long, undivided, oblong-lanceolate, heart-shaped at base, fruit-dots linear, elongated. Growing among the fragments of limestone cliffs. Very rare. P. 150.

## 36. VIRGINIA CHAIN FERN

*Woodwardia Virginica*

Large, fronds once-pinnate, pinnæ pinnatifid, fruit-dots oblong, in chain-like rows parallel and near to the midrib, confluent when ripe. In swamps. P. 156.

# GROUP VI

## FERTILE AND STERILE FRONDS LEAF-LIKE AND USUALLY SIMILAR, FRUIT-DOTS ROUND

## 37. NEW YORK FERN

*Aspidium Noveboracense*

Usually rather tall, fronds once-pinnate, with deeply pinnatifid pinnæ, tapering both ways from the middle, margins of fertile fronds not revolute. In woods and open meadows. P. 159.

## 38. MARSH FERN

*Aspidium Thelypteris*

Usually rather tall, fronds once-pinnate, with pinnæ deeply pinnatifid, scarcely narrower at the base than at the middle, veins forked, fertile fronds noticeable from their *strongly revolute* margins. In wet woods and open swamps. P. 160.

## 39. MASSACHUSETTS FERN

*Aspidium simulatum*

Close to preceding species, rather tall, fronds once-pinnate, with pinnatifid pinnæ little or not at all narrowed at base, veins not forked, margin of fertile frond slightly revolute. In wooded swamps. P. 164.

**47**

## CHRISTMAS FERN

*Aspidium acrostichoides*

[See No. 17]

### 40. SPINULOSE WOOD FERN

*Aspidium spinulosum var. intermedium*

Very common, usually but not always large, fronds oblong-ovate, 2–3 pinnate, lowest pinnæ unequally triangular-ovate, lobes of pinnæ thorny-toothed. In woods everywhere. P. 166.

### 41. BOOTT'S SHIELD FERN

*Aspidium Boottii*

From one and a half to more than three feet high. Sterile fronds smaller and simpler than the fertile, nearly or quite twice-pinnate, the lowest pinnæ triangular-ovate, upper longer and narrower, pinnules oblong-ovate, sharply thorny-toothed. In moist woods. P. 168.

### 42. CRESTED SHIELD FERN

*Aspidium cristatum*

Usually rather large, fronds linear-oblong or lanceolate, once pinnate with pinnatifid pinnæ, linear-oblong, fruit-dots between midvein and margin. In swamps. P. 170.

### 43. CLINTON'S WOOD FERN

*Aspidium cristatum, var. Clintonianum*

In every way larger than preceding species, fronds usually twice-pinnate, pinnæ *broadest at base*, fruit-dots near the midvein. In swampy woods. P. 172.

### 44. GOLDIE'S FERN

*Aspidium Goldianum*

Large, fronds broadly ovate or the fertile ovate-oblong, once-pinnate with pinnatifid pinnæ, pinnæ *broadest in the middle*, fruit-dots very near the midvein. In rich woods. P. 175.

48

## 45. EVERGREEN WOOD FERN

*Aspidium marginale*

Very common, usually rather large, smooth, somewhat leathery, fronds ovate oblong, 1–2 pinnate, fruit-dots large, distinct, close to the margin. In rocky woods. P. 176.

## 46. FRAGRANT SHIELD FERN

*Aspidium fragrans*

Small, fragrant, fronds once-pinnate, with pinnatifid pinnæ, stalk and rachis chaffy, fruit-dots large. On rocks northward, especially near waterfalls. P. 178.

## 47. BRAUN'S HOLLY FERN

*Aspidium aculeatum var. Braunii*

Rather large, fronds oblong-lanceolate, twice-pinnate, pinnules sharply toothed, covered with long, soft hairs, fruit-dots small. In deep, rocky woods. P. 182.

## 48. COMMON POLYPODY

*Polypodium vulgare*

Usually small, fronds somewhat leathery, narrowly oblong, fruit-dots large, round, uncovered, half-way between midvein and margin. On rocks. P. 184.

## HAY-SCENTED FERN

*Dicksonia pilosiuscula*

[See No. 23]

## 49. LONG BEECH FERN

*Phegopteris polypodioides*

Medium-sized, fronds downy, triangular, longer than broad, once-pinnate, pinnæ pinnatifid; lowest pair deflexed and standing forward. In moist woods and on the banks of streams. P. 187.

## 50. BROAD BEECH FERN

*Phegopteris hexagonoptera*

Larger than the preceding species, fronds triangular, as broad or broader than long, once-pinnate, pinnæ pinnatifid, lowest pair very large, basal segments of pinnæ forming a continuous, many-angled wing along the rachis. In dry woods and on hill-sides. P. 188.

## 51. OAK FERN

*Phegopteris Dryopteris*

Medium-sized, fronds thin and delicate, broadly triangular, spreading, ternate, the three divisions stalked, each division pinnate, pin næ pinnatifid. In moist woods. P. 190.

## 52. BULBLET BLADDER FERN

*Cystopteris bulbifera*

Fronds delicate, elongated, tapering above from a broad base, 2-3 pinnate or pinnatifid, bearing fleshy bulblets beneath. On wet rocks, preferring limestone. P. 194.

## 53. COMMON BLADDER FERN

*Cystopteris fragilis*

Medium-sized, fronds thin, oblong-lanceolate, 2–3 pinnate or pinnatifid. On rocks and in moist woods. P. 198.

## 54. RUSTY WOODSIA

*Woodsia Ilvensis*

Small, more or less covered with rusty hairs, fronds lanceolate, once-pinnate, pinnæ pinnatifid. On exposed rocks. P. 200.

## 55. BLUNT-LOBED WOODSIA

*Woodsia obtusa*

Small, slightly downy, fronds broadly lanceolate, nearly twice-pinnate. On rocks. P. 202.

## 56. NORTHERN WOODSIA

*Woodsia hyperborea*

Very small, smooth or nearly so, fronds narrowly oblong-lance-
late, once-pinnate, pinnæ cordate-ovate or triangular-ovate, 5–7
lobed. On moist rocks. P. 203.

## 57. SMOOTH WOODSIA

*Woodsia glabella*

Very small, smooth throughout and delicate, fronds linear, once-
pinnate, pinnæ roundish ovate, lobed. On moist rocks. P. 206.

# FERN DESCRIPTIONS

*"Nature made a fern for pure leaves."—Thoreau*

# GROUP I

## 1. SENSITIVE FERN

*Onoclea sensibilis*

Newfoundland to Florida, in wet meadows.

*Sterile fronds.*—One or two inches to three feet high, broadly triangular, deeply cut into somewhat oblong, wavy-toothed divisions, the lower ones almost reaching the midrib, the upper ones less deeply cut; *stalk* long.

*Fertile fronds.*—Quite unlike the sterile fronds and shorter, erect, rigid, contracted; *pinnules* rolled up into dark-green, berry-like bodies which hold the spore-cases; appearing in June or July.

This is one of our commonest ferns, growing in masses along the roadside and in wet meadows. Perfectly formed sterile fronds are found of the tiniest dimensions. Again the plant holds its own among the largest and most effective ferns. From its creeping rootstock rise the scattered fronds

54

which at times wear very light and delicate shades of green. There is nothing, however, specially fragile in the plant's appearance, and one is struck by the inappropriateness of its title. It is probable that this arose from its sensitiveness to early frosts.

Though one hesitates to differ from Dr. Eaton, who described the fertile fronds as "nearly black in color" and said that they were "not very common," and that a young botanist might "search in vain for them for a long time," my own experience has been that the fresh ones are

Sensitive Fern

very evidently green and neither scarce nor specially inconspicuous.

I have found these fertile fronds apparently full-grown in June, though usually they are assigned to a much later date. They remain standing, brown and dry, long after they have sown their spores, side by side with the fresh fronds of the following summer.

Detail *a* in Plate I represents the so-called *var. obtusilobata.* This is a form midway between the fruiting and the non-fruiting fronds. It may be looked for in situations where the fern has suffered some injury or deprivation.

### 2. OSTRICH FERN

*Onoclea Struthiopteris*

Nova Scotia to New Jersey, along streams and in moist woods. Growing in a crown, two to ten feet high.

*Sterile fronds.*—Broadly lance-shaped, once-pinnate ; *pinnæ* divided into narrowly oblong segments which do not reach the midvein ; *stalk* short, deeply channelled in front.

*Fertile fronds.*—Quite unlike the sterile fronds, growing in the centre of the crown formed by the sterile fronds, shorter, erect, rigid, with green, necklace-like pinnæ which hold the spore-cases ; appearing in July.

I first found this plant at its best on the shore of the Hoosick River in Rensselaer County, N. Y. We had crossed a field dotted with fragrant heaps of hay and blazing in the midsummer sun, and had entered the cool shade of the trees which border the river, when suddenly I saw before me a group of ferns of tropical beauty and luxuriance. Great

PLATE I

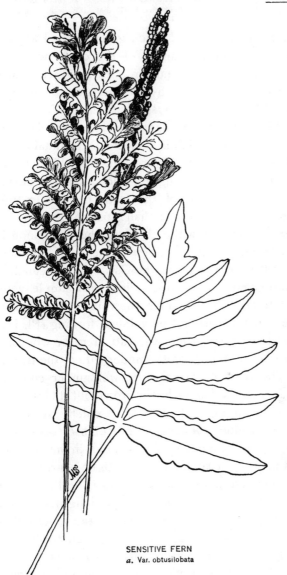

SENSITIVE FERN
*a.* Var. obtusilobata

plume-like fronds of a rich green arched above my head. From the midst of the circle which they formed sprang the shorter, dark, rigid fruit-clusters. I was fairly startled by the unexpected beauty and regal bearing of the Ostrich Fern.

This magnificent plant luxuriates especially in the low, rich soil which is subject to an annual overflow from our northern rivers. Its vase-like masses of foliage somewhat suggest the Cinnamon Fern, but the fertile fronds of the Ostrich Fern mature in July, some weeks later than those of its rival. They are dark-green, while those of the Cinnamon Fern are golden-brown. Should there be no fruiting fronds upon the plant, the Ostrich Fern can be distinguished by the free veins with simple veinlets (Plate II, *a*) of its pinnæ, the veins of the Cinnamon Fern being free and its veinlets forking (Pl. III, *a*), and by the absence of the tuft of rusty wool at the base of the pinnæ on the under side of the frond.

The Ostrich Fern does so well under cultivation that there is danger lest it crowd out its less aggressive neighbors. It propagates chiefly by means of underground runners. Mr. Robinson describes a specimen which he had planted in his out-door fernery that crawled under a tight board fence and reappeared in the garden of his neighbor, who was greatly astonished and equally delighted so unexpectedly to become the owner of the superb plant.

The Ostrich Fern, like its kinsman the Sensitive Fern, occasionally gives birth to fronds which are midway between its fruiting and its non-fruiting

PLATE II

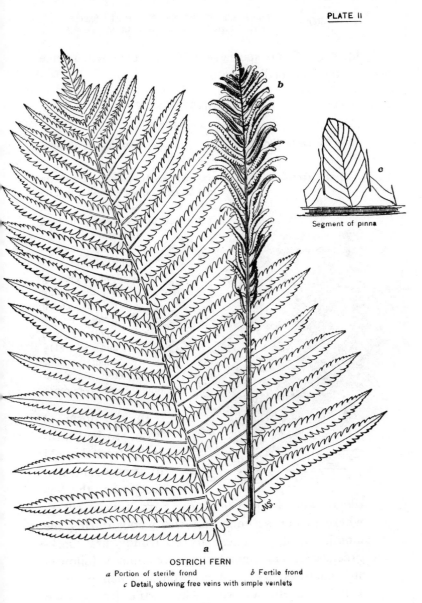

Segment of pinna

**OSTRICH FERN**

*a* Portion of sterile frond          *b* Fertile frond
*c* Detail, showing free veins with simple veinlets

59

forms. This is specially liable to occur when some injury has befallen the plant.

### 3. CINNAMON FERN

*Osmunda cinnamomea*

Nova Scotia to Florida, in swampy places. Growing in a crown, one to five feet high.

*Sterile fronds.*—Broadly lance-shaped, once-pinnate; *pinnæ* cut into broadly oblong divisions that do not reach the midvein, each pinna with a tuft of rusty wool at its base beneath.

*Fertile fronds.*—Quite unlike the sterile fronds, growing in the centre of the crown formed by the sterile fronds and usually about the same height; erect, with cinnamon-colored spore-cases.

In the form of little croziers, protected from the cold by wrappings of rusty wool, the fertile fronds of the Cinnamon Fern appear everywhere in our swamps and wet woods during the month of May. These fertile fronds, first dark-green, later cinnamon-brown, are quickly followed and encircled by the sterile ones, which grow in a tall, graceful crown. The fertile fronds soon

PLATE III

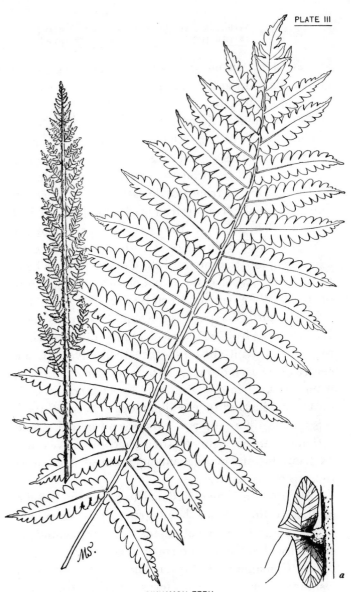

### CINNAMON FERN
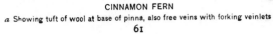
*a* Showing tuft of wool at base of pinna, also free veins with forking veinlets

wither, and, during the summer, may be found either clinging to the stalks of the sterile fronds or lying on the ground.

The Cinnamon Fern is often confused with the Ostrich Fern. When either plant is in fruit there is no excuse for this mistake, as the cinnamon-colored spore-cases of the former appear in May, while the dark-green fertile fronds of the latter do not ripen till July. When the fruiting fronds are absent the forked veinlets (Plate III, *a*) of the Cinnamon Fern contrast with the simple veinlets of the other plant (Plate II, *a*). Then, too, the pinnæ of the Cinnamon Fern bear tufts of rusty wool at the base beneath, the remnants of the woolly garments worn by the young fronds.

The plant is a superb one when seen at its best. Its tall sterile fronds curve gracefully outward, while the slender fruit-clusters erect themselves in the centre of the rich crown. In unfavorable conditions, when growing in dry meadows, for instance, like all the Osmundas, and indeed like most growing things, it is quite a different plant. Its green fronds become stiff and stunted, losing all their graceful curves, and its fruit-clusters huddle among them as if anxious to keep out of sight.

*Var. frondosa* is an occasional form in which some of the fruiting fronds have green, leaf-like pinnæ below. These abnormal fronds are most abundant on land which has been burned over.

The Cinnamon Fern is a member of the group of Osmundas, or "flowering ferns," as they are sometimes called, not of course because they really flower,

but because their fruiting fronds are somewhat
flower-like in appearance. There are three species of
*Osmunda :* the Cinnamon Fern, *O. cinnamomea;* the
Royal Fern, *O. regalis;* and the Interrupted Fern, *O.
Claytoniana.* All three are beautiful and striking
plants, producing their spores in May or June, and
conspicuous by reason of their luxuriant growth and
flower-like fruit clusters.

The Osmundas are easily cultivated, and group
themselves effectively in shaded corners of the
garden. They need plenty of water, and thrive best
in a mixture of swamp-muck and fine loam.

### 4. CURLY GRASS

*Schizæa pusilla*

Pine barrens of New Jersey.

*Sterile fronds.*—Hardly an inch long, linear, slender, flattened,
curly.

*Fertile fronds.*—Taller than the sterile fronds (three or four
inches in height), slender, with from four to six pairs of fruit-bearing
pinnæ in September.

Save in the herbarium I have never seen this very
local little plant, which is found in certain parts of
New Jersey. Gray assigns it to "low grounds, pine
barrens," while Dr. Eaton attributes it to the "drier
parts of sphagnous swamps among white cedars."
In my lack of personal knowledge of *Schizæa*, I
venture to quote from that excellent little quarterly, the *Fern Bulletin,* the following passage from an

article by Mr. C. F. Saunders on *Schizæa pusilla* at
home:

"S. pusilla was first collected early in this century
at Quaker Bridge, N. J., about thirty-five miles east
of Philadelphia. The spot is a desolate-looking
place in the wildest of the 'pine barrens,' where a
branch of the Atsion River flows through marshy
lowlands and cedar swamps. Here, amid sedge-
grasses, mosses, Lycopodiums, Droseras, and wild
cranberry vines, the little treasure has been collected; but, though I have hunted for it more than
once, my eyes have never been sharp enough to
detect its fronds in that locality. In October of
last year, however, a friend guided me to another
place in New Jersey where he knew it to be growing, and there we found it. It was a small open
spot in the pine barrens, low and damp. In the
white sand grew patches of low grasses, mosses,
Lycopodium Carolinianum, L. inundatum, and
Pyxidanthera barbulata, besides several smaller
ericaceous plants and some larger shrubs, such as
scrub-oaks, sumacs, etc. Close by was a little
stream, and just beyond that a bog. Although we
knew that the Schizæa grew within a few feet of
the path in which we stood, it required the closest
sort of a search, with eyes at the level of our knees,
before a specimen was detected. The sterile fronds
(curled like corkscrews) grew in little tufts, and
were more readily visible than the fertile spikes,
which were less numerous, and, together with the
slender stipes, were of a brown color, hardly dis-

PLATE IV

CURLY GRASS

tinguishable from the capsules of the mosses, and
the maturing stems of the grasses which grew all
about. Lying flat on the earth, with face within a
few inches of the ground, was found the most satisfactory plan of search. Down there all the indi-
vidual plants looked bigger, and a sidelong glance
brought the fertile clusters more prominently into
view. When the sight got accustomed to the miniature jungle quite a number of specimens were found,
but the fern could hardly be said to be plentiful,
and all that we gathered were within a radius of a
couple of yards. This seems, indeed, to be one of
those plants whose whereabouts is oftenest revealed
by what we are wont to term a 'happy accident,'
as, for instance, when we are lying stretched on the
ground resting, or as we stoop at lunch to crack an
egg on the toe of our shoe. I know of one excellent collector who spent a whole day looking for it
diligently in what he thought to be a likely spot,
but without success, when finally, just before the
time for return came, as he was half crouching on
the ground, scarcely thinking now of Schizæa, its
fronds suddenly flashed upon his sight, right at his
feet. The sterile fronds of Schizæa pusilla are evergreen, so that the collector may, perhaps, most readily detect it in winter, selecting days for his search
when the earth is pretty clear of snow. The surrounding vegetation being at that time dead, the
little corkscrew-like fronds stand out more prominently."

# GROUP II

FERTILE FRONDS PARTIALLY LEAF-LIKE, THE FERTILE
PORTION UNLIKE THE REST OF THE FROND

## 5. ROYAL FERN. FLOWERING FERN

*Osmunda regalis*

New Brunswick to Florida, in swampy places.   Two to five feet
high, occasionally taller.

*Sterile fronds.*—Twice-pinnate, *pinnæ* cut into oblong pinnules.
*Fertile fronds.*—Leaf-like below, *sporangia* forming bright-
brown clusters at their summits.

Perhaps this Royal or Flowering Fern is the
most beautiful member of a singularly beautiful
group.   When its smooth, pale - green sterile
fronds, grown to their full height, form a graceful crown which encircles the fertile fronds, it is
truly a regal-looking plant.   These fertile fronds

are leaf-
like be-
low, and
are tipped
above with their flower-like
fruit-clusters.

Like its kinsmen, the Royal
Fern appears in May in our
wet woods and fields. The
delicate little croziers uncurl
with dainty grace, the plants
which grow in the open among
the yellow stars of the early
crow-foot, and the white clusters of the spring cress
being so tinged with red
that they suffuse the
meadows with warm
color.

Though one of our
tallest ferns, with us it
never reaches the ten or
eleven feet with which it is
credited in Great Britain.
The tallest plants I have
found fall short of six feet.
Occasionally we see large
tracts of land covered with
mature plants that lack a
foot or more of the two feet
given as the minimum height. This tendency to

Royal Fern

PLATE V

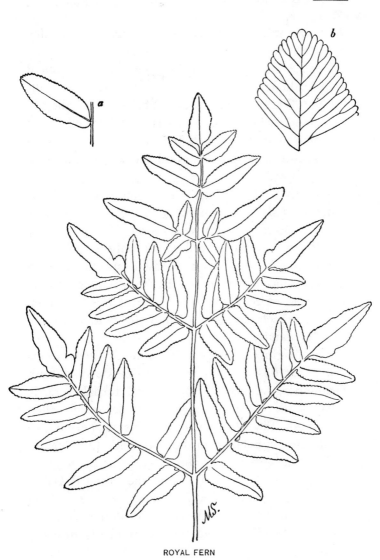

ROYAL FERN

*a* Pinnule of Royal Fern          *b* Showing veining

depauperization one notices especially in dry marshes near the sea.

To the Royal Fern the old herbalists attributed many valuable qualities.  One old writer, who calls it the " Water Fern," says : " This hath all the virtues mentioned in other ferns, and is much more effective than they both for inward and outward griefs, and is accounted good for wounds, bruises, and the like."

The title " flowering fern " sometimes misleads those who are so unfamiliar with the habits of ferns as to imagine that they ever flower.  That it really is descriptive was proved to me only a few weeks ago when I received a pressed specimen of a fertile frond accompanied by the request to inform the writer as to the name of the flower inclosed, which seemed to him to belong to the Sumach family.

The origin of the generic name *Osmunda* seems somewhat obscure.  It is said to be derived from Osmunder, the Saxon Thor.  In his Herbal Gerarde tells us that *Osmunda regalis* was formerly called " Osmund, the Waterman," in allusion, perhaps, to its liking for a home in the marshes.  One legend claims that a certain Osmund, living at Loch Tyne, saved his wife and child from the inimical Danes by hiding them upon an island among masses of flowering ferns, and that in after years the child so shielded named the stately plants after her father.

The following lines from Wordsworth point to still another origin of the generic name :

> " — often, trifling with a privilege
> Alike indulged to all, we paused, one now,
> And now the other, to point out, perchance
> To pluck, some flower, or water-weed, too fair
> Either to be divided from the place
> On which it grew, or to be left alone
> To its own beauty.   Many such there are,
> Fair ferns and flowers, and chiefly that tall fern,
> So stately, of the Queen Osmunda named ;
> Plant lovelier, in its own retired abode
> On Grasmere's beach, than Naiad by the side
> Of Grecian brook, or Lady of the Mere,
> Sole-sitting by the shores of old romance."

The Royal Fern may be cultivated easily in deep mounds of rich soil shielded somewhat from the sun.

## 6. INTERRUPTED FERN

*Osmunda Claytoniana*

Newfoundland to North Carolina, in swampy places. Two to
four feet high.

*Sterile fronds.*—Oblong-lanceolate, once-pinnate, *pinnæ* cut into
oblong, obtuse divisions, *without* a tuft of wool at the base of each
pinna.

*Fertile fronds.*—Taller than the sterile, leaf-like above and
below, some of the middle pinnæ fruit-bearing.

The Interrupted Fern makes its appearance in
the woods and meadows and along the roadsides in
May. It fruits as it unfolds.

At first the fruiting pinnæ are almost black. Later
they become golden-green, and after the spores are
discharged they turn brown. They are noticeable
all summer, and serve to identify the plant at once.

In the absence of the fertile fronds it is often
difficult to distinguish between the Cinnamon Fern
and the Interrupted Fern.

The sterile fronds of the Interrupted Fern are
usually less erect, curving outward much more
noticeably than those of the Cinnamon Fern. Then,
too, its pinnæ are cut into segments that are more obtuse, and the whole effect of the frond is more stubby.

But the most distinguishing feature of all is the
tuft of rusty wool which clings to the base of each
pinna of the sterile fronds of the Cinnamon Fern.
These tufts we do not find in the Interrupted Fern,
though both plants come into the world warmly
wrapped in wool.

The Interrupted Fern is a peculiarly graceful plant.

72

PLATE VI

**INTERRUPTED FERN**

*a* Clusters of sporangia        *b* Showing veining

Its fertile
fronds, stand-
ing quite erect
below but curving
outward above the
fruiting pinnæ, are
set in a somewhat
shallow vase formed
by the sterile fronds,
which fall away in
every direction.

In the fall the
fronds turn yel-
low, and
at times
are so
brilliant
t h a t
t h e y
flood the
w o o d s
with gold-
en light.

Like the
other Os-
mundas,
the Inter-
rupted
Fern is
easily cul-
tivated.

Interrupted Fern

## 7. CLIMBING FERN. CREEPING FERN. HARTFORD FERN

*Lygodium palmatum*

Massachusetts and southward, in moist
   thickets and open woods. Stalks
   slender and twining.

*Fronds.*—Climbing and twining, one
to three feet long, divided into lobed,
rounded, heart - shaped, short - stalked
segments ; *fruit - clusters*, growing at
the summit of the frond, ripening in
September.

The Climbing Fern is still found
occasionally in moist thickets and
open woods from Massachusetts southward,
but at one time it was picked so reck-
lessly for decorative purposes that it was almost
exterminated.

In 1869 the legislature of Connecticut passed for
its protection a special law which was embodied in
the revision of the statutes of 1875, "perhaps the

only instance in statute law," Dr. Eaton remarks, "where a plant has received special legal protection solely on account of its beauty."

I have never seen the plant growing, but remember that when a child my home in New York was abundantly decorated with the pressed fronds which

had been brought from Hartford for the purpose. Even in that lifeless condition their grace and beauty made a deep impression on my mind.

Mr. Saunders has described it as he found it growing in company with *Schizæa*, in the New Jersey pine barrens :

Part of fertile pinnule

" Lygodium palmatum . . . is one of the loveliest of American plants, with twining stem adorned with palmate leaflets, bearing small resemblance to the popular idea of a fern. It loves the shaded, mossy banks of the quiet streams whose cool, clear, amber waters, murmuring over beds of pure white sand, are so characteristic of the pine country. There the graceful fronds are to be found, sometimes clambering a yard high over the bushes and cat-briers ; sometimes trailing down the bank until their tips touch the surface of the water.

" The Lygodium is reckoned among the rare plants of the region—though often growing in good-sized patches when found at all—and is getting rarer. Many of the localities which knew it once now know it no more, both because of the depredations of ruthless collectors, and, to some extent, probably, the ravages of fire. The plant is in its prime in early fall, but may be looked for up to the time of killing frosts."

## 8. ADDER'S TONGUE

*Ophioglossum vulgatum*

Canada to New Jersey and Kentucky, in moist meadows. Two inches to one foot high.

*Sterile portion.*—An ovate, fleshy leaf.
*Fertile portion.*—A simple spike, usually long-stalked.

The unprofessional fern collector is likely to agree with Gray in considering the Adder's Tongue "not common." Many botanists, however, believe the plant to be "overlooked rather than rare." In an article on *O. vulgatum*, which appeared some years ago in the *Fern Bulletin*, Mr. A. A. Eaton writes:

" Previous to 1895 Ophioglossum vulgatum was unknown to me, and was considered very rare, only two localities being known in Essex County, Mass. Early in the year a friend gave me two specimens. From these I got an idea of how the thing looked. On the 11th of last July, while collecting Habenaria lacera in a 'bound-out' mowing field, I was delighted to notice a spike of fruit in the grass. A search revealed about sixty, just right to collect, with many unfruitful specimens. A few days later,

77

while raking in a similar locality, I found several,
within a stone's throw of the house, demonstrating
again the well-known fact that a thing once seen is
easily discovered again.   On the 23d of last August,
while riding on my bicycle, I noticed a field that
appeared to be the right locality, and an investigation showed an abundance of them.   I subsequently
found it in another place.   This year, on May 28th,
I found it in another locality just as it was coming
up, and I have since found three others.   I con-
sider it abundant here, only appearing rare because
growing hidden in fine grass in old mowing fields,
after the red top and timothy have died out, and the
finer species of Carex are coming in.   A good in-
dex plant is the Habenaria quoted.   I have never
found it except when associated with this plant,
on a cold, heavy soil.   The leaf is usually hidden,
or, if not, is easily passed by for Maianthemum or
Pogonia."

In the "Grete Herbal" of Gerarde we read that
"the leaves of Adder's Tongue stamped in a stone
mortar, and boiled in oyle olive unto the consump-
tion of the juice, and until the herbs be dried and
parched and then strained, will yeelde most excellent
greene oyle or rather a balsame for greene wounds
comparable to oyle of St. John's-wort if it do not
farre surpasse it."

It is said that "Adder's Spear Ointment," made
from the fresh fronds of this plant is still used for
wounds in English villages.

The Adder's Tongue was believed formerly to

PLATE VII

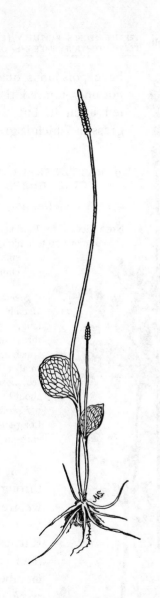

ADDER'S TONGUE

have poisonous qualities, which
not only injured the cattle that
fed upon it, but destroyed the
grass in which it grew.

### 9. RATTLESNAKE FERN. VIR-
### GINIA GRAPE FERN

*Botrychium Virginianum*

Nova Scotia to Florida, in rich woods.
One or two feet high, at times much
smaller, when it be-
comes *B. gracile.*

*Sterile portion.*—
Usually broader than
long, spreading, with
three main divisions
which are cut into many
smaller segments, thin,
set close to the stem
about half way up.
*Fertile portion.*—
Long-stalked, more than
once-pinnate.

On our rambles
through the woods
we are more likely
to encounter the
Rattlesnake Fern
than any other
member of the *Bo-
trychium* group. It
fruits in early sum-

Rattlesnake Fern

80

mer, but the withered fertile portion may be found upon the plant much later in the year. Its frequent companions are the Spinulose Shield Fern, the Christmas Fern, the Silvery Spleenwort, and the Maidenhair.

### 10. TERNATE GRAPE FERN

*Botrychium ternatum* or *dissectum*

Nova Scotia to Florida, in moist meadows.    A few inches to more than a foot high.

*Sterile portion.*—Broadly triangular, the three main divisions cut again into many segments, on a separate stalk from near the base of the plant, fleshy.
*Fertile portion.*—Erect, usually considerably taller than non-fruiting segment, more than once-pinnate.

Sporangia of Botrychium

Of late some doubt has existed as to whether *B. ternatum* has been actually found in this country, although the standard Floras give no evidence of this uncertainty. Dr. Underwood is convinced that the true *B. ternatum* is found only in Japan and China, and that our species is really *B. dissectum*, a species, not a variety. He says that this species is very common in the vicinity of New York City, and thence southward and westward; that it is also found in various parts of New England; that it reaches its fullest development in moist,

81

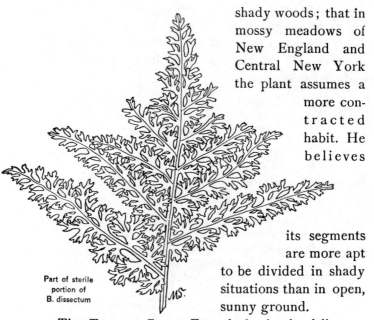

Part of sterile
portion of
B. dissectum

shady woods; that in mossy meadows of New England and Central New York the plant assumes a more contracted habit. He believes its segments are more apt to be divided in shady situations than in open, sunny ground. The Ternate Grape Fern fruits in the fall.

## 11. LITTLE GRAPE FERN

*Botrychium simplex*

Canada to Maryland, in moist woods and in fields. Two to four inches high, rarely a little taller.

*Sterile portion.*—Somewhat oblong, more or less lobed, occasionally 3–7 divided, usually short-stalked from near the middle of the plant, thick and fleshy.

*Fertile portion.*—Either simple or once or twice-pinnate, taller than the sterile portion.

This little plant is sufficiently rare to rejoice the heart of the fern hunter who is so fortunate as to

PLATE VI

**TERNATE GRAPE FERN**

stumble upon it by chance or to trace it to its chosen haunts.

It is generally considered an inhabitant of moist woods and meadows, though Mr. Pringle describes it as "abundantly scattered over Vermont, its habitat usually poor soil, especially knolls of hill pastures," and Mr. Dodge assigns it to "dry fields." It fruits in May or June.

### 12. MOONWORT

*Botrychium Lunaria*

Newfoundland to Connecticut and Central New York, in dry pastures. Three inches to nearly one foot high. A very fleshy plant.

*Sterile portion.*—Oblong, cut into several fan-shaped fleshy divisions, growing close to the stem about the middle of the plant.

*Fertile portion.*—Branching, long-stalked, usually the same height as or taller than the sterile portion.

The Moonwort is another of our rare little plants. It grows usually in dry pastures, fruiting in July.

Formerly it was accredited with various magic powers. Gathered by moonlight, it was said to "do wonders." The English poet Drayton refers to the Moonwort as "Lunary"·

> "Then sprinkled she the juice of rue
> With nine drops of the midnight dew
> From Lunary distilling."

Gerarde mentions its use by alchemists, who called it Martagon. In the work of Coles, an early writer on plants, we read: "It is said, yea, and believed by many that Moonwort will open the

84

PLATE IX

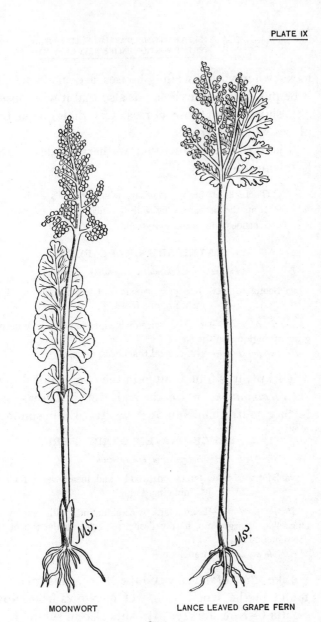

MOONWORT          LANCE LEAVED GRAPE FERN

locks wherewith dwelling-houses are made fast, if it be put into the keyhole ; as also that it will loosen . . . shoes from those horses' feet that go on the places where it grows."

It is to the Moonwort that Withers alludes in the following lines :

> " There is an herb, some say, whose vertue's such
> It in the pasture, only with a touch
> Unshoes the new-shod steed."

### 13. MATRICARY GRAPE FERN

*Botrychium matricariæfolium*

Nova Scotia to New Jersey, in woods and wet meadows. Two inches to one foot high.

*Sterile portion.*—Once or twice divided, sometimes very fleshy, growing high up on the stem.

*Fertile portion.*—With several branched pinnæ.

This plant is found, often in the companionship of *B. Virginianum*, in woods and wet meadows, not farther south than New Jersey. It fruits in summer.

### 14. LANCE-LEAVED GRAPE FERN

*Botrychium lanceolatum*

Nova Scotia to New Jersey, in woods and meadows. Two to nine inches high.

*Sterile portion.*—Triangular, twice-pinnatifid, with somewhat lance-shaped segments, hardly fleshy, set close to the top of the common stalk.

*Fertile portion.*—Branching.

Like the Matricary Grape Fern, this plant is found in the woods and wet meadows from Nova Scotia to New Jersey. It fruits also in summer.

86

# GROUP III

## FERTILE FRONDS UNIFORMLY SOMEWHAT LEAF-LIKE IN APPEARANCE, YET DIFFERING NOTICEABLY FROM STERILE FRONDS

### 15. SLENDER CLIFF BRAKE

*Pellæa gracilis* (*P. Stelleri*)

Labrador to Pennsylvania, usually on sheltered rocks, preferring limestone. Two to five inches long, with straw-colored or pale-brown stalks, slightly chaffy below.

*Fronds.*—Delicate, with few pinnæ; *pinnæ*, the lower ones once or twice parted into 3–5 divisions, those of the fertile frond oblong or linear-oblong, sparingly incised, of the sterile frond ovate or obovate, toothed or incised; *sporangia* bordering the pinnæ of the fertile frond, covered by a broad and usually continuous general *indusium*, formed by the reflexed margin of the *pinnule*.

The first time I found the Slender Cliff Brake was one July day in Central New York, under the kind guidance of an enthusiastic fern collector. A rather perilous climb along the sides of a thickly wooded glen brought us to a spot where our only security lay in clinging to the trees, which, like our-

87

selves, had obtained doubtful standing-room. In a pocket in the limestone just above us I was shown a very brown and withered little plant which only the closest scrutiny in combination with a certain amount of foreknowledge could identify as the Slender Cliff Brake. The season had been a dry one and the plant had perished, I fancy, for lack of water, in spite of the stream which plunged from the top of the cliffs close by, almost near enough, it

seemed to me, to moisten with its spray our hot cheeks.

Later in the season I found more promising though not altogether satisfactory specimens of this plant growing in other rocky crevices of the same deep glen, in the neighborhood of the Maidenhair Spleenwort, the Walking Leaf, and the

Portion of
fertile frond

Bulblet Bladder Fern.

My sister tells me that late in August on the cliffs which border the St. Lawrence River, refreshed by the myriad streams which leap or trickle down their sides, under the hanging roots of trees, close to clusters of quivering harebells and pale tufts of the Brittle Bladder Fern, the Slender Cliff Brake grows in profusion, its delicate fronds rippling over one another so closely that at times they give the effect of a long, luxuriant moss. On most occasions, in these soft beds of foliage, she found the fertile fronds, which are far more slender and unusual looking than the sterile, largely predominating, though at times a patch would be

made up chiefly of the sterile fronds.   These somewhat resemble the Brittle Bladder Fern in whose
company they are seen so often.

Slender Cliff Brake

89

## 16. PURPLE CLIFF BRAKE

*Pellæa atropurpurea*

Canada to Georgia and westward, usually on limestone cliffs; with
wiry purplish stalks.

*Fertile fronds.*—Six to twenty inches high, leathery, bluish-green,
pale underneath, once, or below twice, pinnate; *pinnæ*, upper ones
long and narrow, lower ones usually with one to four pairs of
broadly linear *pinnules; sporangia* bordering the pinnæ, bright
brown at maturity; *indusium* formed by the reflexed margin of the
frond.

*Sterile fronds.*—Usually much smaller than the fertile and less
abundant; *pinnæ* oblong, entire, or slightly toothed.

The Purple Cliff Brake is one of the plants that rejoice in un-get-at-able and perilous situations. Although its range is wider than that of many ferns,
this choice of inconvenient localities, joined to the
fact that it is not a common plant, renders it likely
that unless you pay it the compliment of a special
expedition in its honor you will never add it to the
list of your fern acquaintances.

But when all is said we are inestimably in debt to
the plants so rare or so exclusive as to entice us out
of our usual haunts into theirs. Not only do they
draw us away from our books, out of our houses,
but off the well-known road and the trodden path
into unfamiliar woods which stand ready to reveal
fresh treasures, across distant pastures where the
fragrant wind blows away the memory of small
anxieties, up into the hills from whose summits we
get new views.

Although the Purple Cliff Brake grows, I believe,

PLATE X

**PURPLE CLIFF BRAKE**
*a* Portion of fertile frond

within fifteen miles of my home in Albany, I never
saw the plant until this summer some hundred miles
nearer the centre of the State.   During a morning
call I chanced to mention that I was anxious to find
two or three ferns which were said to grow in the
neighborhood.   My hostess told me that twenty-five
years before, on some limestone cliffs about eight
miles away, she had found two unknown ferns which
had been classified and labelled by a botanical friend.
Excusing herself she left me and soon returned with
carefully pressed specimens of the Purple Cliff
Brake and the little Rue Spleenwort, the two ferns
I was most eager to find.   Such moments as I experienced then of long-deferred but peculiar satisfaction go far toward making one an apostle of
hobbies.   My pleasure was increased by the kind
offer to guide me to the spot which had yielded the
specimens.

One morning soon after we were set down at the
little railway station from which we purposed to
walk to the already-mentioned cliffs.   We were not
without misgivings as we followed an indefinite path
across some limestone quarries, for a plant may
easily disappear from a given station in the course of
twenty-five years.   In a few moments the so-called
path disappeared in a fringe of bushes which evidently marked the beginning of a precipitous descent.   Cautiously clinging to whatever we could
lay hold of, bushes, roots of trees or imbedded rocks,
we climbed over the cliff's side, still following the
semblance of a path.   On our left a stream plunged

nearly two hundred feet into the ravine below. For
some distance the eye could follow its silver course,
then it disappeared beneath the arching trees. On
our right, many miles beyond, through the blue haze
which hung over the distant valley, we could see the
lake to which the stream was hurrying.

We could not surrender ourselves with comfort
to the beauty of the outlook, as our surroundings
were not such as to put us altogether at ease. Overhead hung great rocks, so cracked and seamed and
shattered as to threaten a complete downfall, while
beneath our feet the path which led along the face
of the cliff crumbled away, so that it was difficult
in places to obtain any foothold. Having passed
the more perilous spots, however, we became accustomed to the situation and turned our attention to
the unpromising wall of rock which rose beside us.
From its crevices hung graceful festoons of Bulblet
Bladder Fern, and apparently nothing but Bulblet
Bladder Fern. But soon one of the party gave a
cry and pointed in triumph to a bluish-green cluster
of foliage which sprang from a shallow pocket overhead. Even though one had not seen the plant
before, there was no mistaking the wiry purplish
stalks, the leathery, pinnately parted, blue-green
fronds, and, above all, the marginal rows of bright
brown sporangia peculiar to the Purple Cliff Brake.
Soon after we found several other plants, all of them
decidedly scraggly in appearance, with but few
green fronds and many leafless stalks. Occasionally a small sterile frond, with broader, more oblong

93

pinnæ, could be seen, but these were in the minority. A number of very young plants, with little, heart-shaped leaves altogether unlike the mature fronds, were wedged in neighboring crannies.

As our eyes grew more accustomed to the contour and coloring of the cliffs, the success of the day was completed by the discovery of several specimens of the little Rue Spleenwort with tiny fronds flattened against the rock.

When next I saw the Purple Cliff Brake it seemed to me quite a different fern from the rather awkward plant, the mere sight of which I had welcomed so eagerly that any unfavorable criticism of its appearance seems ungrateful.

Again it sprang from limestone cliffs, even more remote and inaccessible though less dangerous than those where I saw it first. These cliffs were so shattered in places that the broken fragments lay in heaps at their base and on the projecting ledges. Here and there a great shaft of rock had broken away and stood like the turret of a castle or the bastion of a fort. Among the shattered fragments high up on the cliff's side the Purple Cliff Brake grew in a luxuriant profusion that was amazing in view of the surroundings. The rigid, erect fronds formed large tufts of greenish-gray foliage that, at a little distance, so blended with their rocky background as to be almost indistinguishable. The fronds usually were much more compound than those I had seen a few weeks before. The separate plants had a vigorous, bushy appearance that did

94

not suggest the same species. Many of the pinnæ were so turned as to display the ripe sporangia, which formed a bright-brown border to the pale, slender divisions. Here, too, the small sterile fronds were very rare.

Growing from the broken rocks in among the Purple Cliff Brake were thrifty little tufts of the Maidenhair Spleenwort. This tiny plant seemed to have forgotten its shyness and to have forsworn its love for moist, shaded, mossy rocks. It ventured boldly out upon these barren cliffs, exposing itself to the fierce glare of the sun and to every blast of wind, and holding itself upright with a saucy self-assurance that seemed strangely at variance with its nature.

Near by a single patch of the Walking Leaf climbed up the face of the cliff, while, perhaps strangest of all, from the decaying trunk of a tree, which lay prostrate among the rocks, sprang a single small but perfect plant of the Ebony Spleenwort, a fern which was a complete stranger in this locality, so far as I could learn.

a.g.s.

More compound frond of Purple Cliff Brake

Sterile frond

95

## 17. CHRISTMAS FERN

*Aspidium acrostichoides (Dryopteris acrostichoides)*

New Brunswick to Florida, in rocky woods. One to two and a half feet high, with very chaffy stalks.

*Fronds.*—Lance-shaped, once-pinnate, fertile fronds contracted toward the summit; *pinnæ* narrowly lance-shaped, half halberd-shaped at the slightly stalked base, bristly-toothed, the upper ones on the fertile fronds contracted and smaller; *fruit-dots* round, close, confluent with age, nearly covering the under surface of the fertile pinnæ; *indusium* orbicular, fixed by the depressed centre.

Of our evergreen ferns this is the best fitted to serve as a decoration in winter. No other fern has

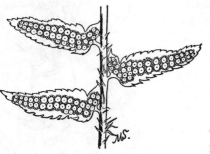

Portion of fertile frond

such deep-green, highly polished fronds. They need only a mixture of red berries to become a close rival to the holly at Christmas time.

Wrapped in a garment of brown scales, the young fronds of the Christmas Fern are sent into the world early in the spring. When we go to the woods in April to look for arbutus, or to listen to the first songs of the robin and the bluebird, we notice that last year's fronds are still fresh and green. Low down among them, curled up like tawny caterpillars, are the young fronds. The arbutus will have made way for pink and blue and white hepaticas, for starry bloodroot, and for tremulous anemones; thrushes and orioles will have joined the robins and the bluebirds before these new-comers present much of an

96

appearance. When the tender, delicately green fronds are first unrolled they contrast strongly with their polished, dark-green, leathery companions.

In this plant the difference is quite conspicuous between the fertile and the sterile fronds. The sterile ones are shorter and apparently broader, while the fertile are tall, slender, and noticeably contracted by the abundantly fruiting pinnæ near the apex.

a.g.s.

Christmas Fern

## 18. NARROW-LEAVED SPLEEN-WORT

*Asplenium angustifolium*

Canada to Kentucky, in moist woods. Two to four feet high.

*Sterile fronds.* — Thin, smooth, lance-shaped, perishable, once-pinnate.

*Fertile fronds.*—Taller, narrower, longer-stalked; *pinnæ* more narrowly lance-shaped than on sterile fronds; *fruit-dots* linear, a row on each side the midvein; *indusium* slightly convex.

If we make an expedition to the woods early in July we may, perhaps, find some plants of the Narrow-leaved Spleenwort. At this season they are specially attractive, with smooth, delicate, pale-green fronds, so recently unfolded as to be full of little undulations, which they lose more or less at maturity, and which are as indicative of youth as the curves and dimples of a baby.

PLATE XI

**NARROW-LEAVED SPLEENWORT**
*a* Magnified pinna of fertile frond

Late in August the plant has reached a stately height, perhaps of three or four feet. The fronds are still smooth and delicate to a degree unusual even in ferns. But they wear a deeper green, and their texture seems a trifle more substantial. Occasionally, though rarely in the deeper woods, we find a frond which is conspicuously longer-stalked, taller, narrower than the others, with pinnæ more distant and more contracted. A glance at its lower surface discovers double rows of brown, linear fruit-dots.

Though one of the largest of its tribe, the Narrow-leaved Spleenwort suggests greater fragility, a keener sensitiveness to uncongenial conditions, than any other of our native ferns. A storm which leaves the other inhabitants of the forest almost untouched beats down its fronds, tender and perishable even in maturity.

This very fragility, accompanied as it is with beauty of form and color, in the midst of the somewhat coarse and hardy growth of the August woods, lends the plant a peculiar charm.

I find it growing beneath great basswoods, lichen-spotted beeches, and sugar maples with trunks branchless for fifty feet, soaring like huge shipmasts into the blue above.

Almost the only flowers in its neighborhood, for in midsummer wood-flowers are rare, are the tiny pink blossoms of the herb Robert, that invincible little plant which never wearies in well-doing, but persists in flowering from June till October, the violet-blue heads of the almost equally untiring self-heal and the yellow pitchers of the pale touch-me-not or jewel-weed. This plant, a close relative of the more southern and better known spotted touch-me-not, grows in great patches almost in the heart of the woods. The lack of flowers is somewhat atoned for by the coral clusters of the red baneberry and the black-spotted, china-like fruit of the white baneberry.

But ferns chiefly abound in these woods. Everywhere I notice the thin, spreading frond and withered fruit-cluster of the Rattlesnake Fern, in my experience the most ubiquitous member of the *Botrychium* group. More or less frequent are graceful crowns of the Spinulose Shield Fern, slender shining fronds of Christmas Fern, dull-green groups of Silvery Spleenwort and stately plumes of Goldie's Fern. As we draw near the wood's border, where the yellow sunlit fields of grain shine between the tall maple shafts, we push aside umbrella-like Brakes. At the very limits of the woods, close against the rails, grows the sweet-scented *Dicksonia*.

## 19. NET-VEINED CHAIN FERN

### *Woodwardia angustifolia*

Swampy places from Maine to Florida, in wet woods near the coast.

*Sterile fronds.*—Twelve to eighteen inches high, pinnatifid with minutely toothed divisions united by a broad wing.

*Fertile fronds.*—Taller than the sterile, once-pinnate; *pinnæ* much contracted; *fruit-dots* in a single row each side of the secondary midribs; *indusium* fixed by its outer margin, opening on the side next the midrib.

The Woodwardias are associated in my mind with sea-air, pine-trees, and the flat, sandy country

near Buzzard's Bay, Mass. Both species were met with in one walk not far from the shore.

A little stream, scarcely more than a ditch, divided an open, sunny meadow from a bit of evergreen wood, and on the steep banks of this runlet grew the bright fronds of *Woodwardia angustifolia*, giving at first glance somewhat the impression of *Onoclea sensibilis*. The fronds of both are described as pinnatifid, and in this *Woodwardia* we find the divisions minutely toothed (*a*), giving them a rough outline which is wanting in *Onoclea sensibilis*. These are the sterile fronds. Among them and taller than they are the fertile fronds with very narrow divisions, covered on the lower side with the chains of fruit-dots (*b*).

PLATE XII

NET-VEINED CHAIN FERN
103

It is a handsome fern and very satisfactory to the novice in fern hunting, because, taking fertile and sterile fronds together, it cannot be confused with any other species.

Crossing the tiny stream, a path dim with the shade of low, dense evergreens and soft and elastic underfoot from their fallen leaves, leads through the woods. Here among the partridge-vine that runs over the rocks, growing from the soft, spongy soil, are groups of the sterile fronds only of this *Woodwardia*, charming little clumps of fresh green that invite one to dig them up and plant them in boxes or baskets for decorative purposes.

# GROUP IV

## 20. BRAKE. BRACKEN. EAGLE FERN

*Pteris aquilina*

Almost throughout North America, in dry, somewhat open places. One to two feet high ordinarily, occasionally much higher.

*Fronds.*—Solitary, one to two feet wide, cut into three primary divisions which are twice-pinnate, widely spreading at the summit of an erect, stout stalk; *sporangia* borne in a continuous line along the lower margin of the frond; *indusium* formed by the reflexed edge of the frond.

Of all ferns the Brake is the most widely distributed. It occurs in one form or another in all parts of the world. With us it grows commonly from one to two feet high, occasionally higher. In Oregon it attains a height of six or seven feet, in the Andes of fourteen feet.

It is a vigorous and often a beautiful and striking plant, growing abundantly on sunny hillsides and in open woods.

In the spring or early summer its solitary spreading frond, light-green and delicate in color, might almost be confused with the Oak Fern. Later its green takes on a dark, dull shade, and its general aspect becomes more hardy than that of any other fern.

The Brake is be-

lieved to be the "fearn" of the early Saxons and to have given this prefix to many English towns and villages, such as Fearnhow or Farnhow, Farningham, etc.

It is one of the few ferns mentioned by name in general literature. In the "Lady of the Lake" it is alluded to in the song of the heir of Armandave:

Brake

> "The heath this night must be my bed,
> The Bracken curtain for my head."

*Pteris esculenta*, a variety of our Brake, is said to have been one of the chief articles of food in New Zealand. It was called "fern-root," and in Dr. Thompson's "Story of New Zealand" is spoken of as follows: "This food is celebrated in song, and the young women, in laying before travellers baskets of cooked fern-root, chant: 'What shall be our food? Shall shellfish and fern-root? That is the root of the earth; that is the food to satisfy a man; the tongues grow by reason of the licking, as if it were the tongue of a dog.'"

The titles Brake and Bracken are not always confined to their lawful owner. Frequently they are applied to any large ferns, such as the Osmundas, or even to such superficially fern-like plants as *Myrica asplenifolia*, the so-called sweet fern.

There is a difference of opinion as to the origin of the plant's scientific name, which signifies eagle

Pinnule of Brake showing
reflexed edges

wing. Some suppose it to be derived from the outline of the heraldic eagle which has been seen by the imaginative in a cross-section of the young stalk. It seems more likely that a resemblance has been fancied between the spreading frond and the plumage of an eagle.

107

The Brake turns brown in autumn, but does not wither away till the following year.

### 21. MAIDENHAIR

*Adiantum pedatum*

Nova Scotia to British Columbia, south to Georgia and Arkansas, in moist woods. Ten to eighteen inches high.

*Fronds.*—Forked at the summit of the slender black and polished stalk, the recurved branches bearing on one side several slender, spreading pinnate divisions; *pinnules* obliquely triangular-oblong; *sporangia* in short fruit-dots on the under margin of a lobe of the frond; *indusium* formed by the reflexed lobe or tooth of the frond.

For purposes of identification it would seem almost superfluous to describe the Maidenhair, a

plant which probably is more generally appreciated than all the rest of the ferns together. Yet, s t r a n g e l y enough, it is confused constantly with other plants and with plants which are not ferns.

Perhaps the early meadow rue is the plant most commonly mistaken for the Maidenhair. While it does not suggest strikingly our eastern fern, its lobed and rounded

**A pinna of Maidenhair**

leaflets bear a likeness to certain species native to other parts of the country, notably to *A. Capillus-Veneris*, the Venus-hair Fern of the southern States.

But it is not easy to convince a friend that he has made a mistake in this regard. You chance to be driving by a bank overgrown with the early meadow rue when he calls your attention to the unusual abundance of Maidenhair in the neighborhood. To his rather indignant surprise you suggest that the plant he saw was not Maidenhair, but the early meadow rue. If he have the least reverence for your botanical attainments he grudgingly admits that possibly it was not the ordinary Maidenhair, but maintains stoutly that it was a more uncommon species which abounds in his especial neighborhood. If truly diplomatic you hold your peace and change the subject, but if possessed by a tormenting love of truth which is always getting you into trouble, you state sadly but firmly that our northeastern States have but one species of Maidenhair, and that

A pinnule of Maidenhair

it is more than improbable that the favored neighborhood of his home (for it is always an unusually rich locality) offers another. The result of this discussion is that mentally you are pronounced both conceited and pig-headed. For a few weeks the plants in question are passed without comment, but by another summer the rich growth of Maidenhair is again proudly exhibited. Only in one way can you save your reputation and possibly convince your friend. When correcting him, if you glibly remark that

*Adiantum pedatum*, our northeastern Maidenhair, is the only species which has been found in this part of the country, that *A. Capillus-Veneris*, the Maidenhair which somewhat resembles the early meadow rue, can hardly be found north of Virginia, while *A. tenerum* is found only in Florida, and *A. emarginatum* is confined to the Pacific coast, you will have redeemed yourself, not

Maidenhair

from the stigma of conceit, far from it, but from that of error. The glib utterance of Latin names is attended with a strange power of silencing your opponent and filling him with a sort of grudging belief in your scientific attainments.

The truth is that the average layman who takes an interest in plants is as sensitive regarding the Maidenhair as he is about his recognition of an orchid. By way of warning what more need be said?

Though the Maidenhair has a wide range and grows abundantly in many localities, it possesses a quality of aloofness which adds to its charm. Even in neighborhoods where it grows profusely, it rarely crowds to the roadside or becomes the companion of your daily walks. Its chosen haunts are dim, moist hollows in the woods or shaded hill-sides sloping to the river. In such retreats you find the feathery fronds tremulous on their black, glistening stalks, and in their neighborhood you find also the very spirit of the woods.

Despite its apparent fragility, the Maidenhair is not difficult to cultivate if provided with sufficient shade and moisture.

## 22. HAIRY LIP FERN

*Cheilanthes vestita* (*C. lanosa*)

Growing on rocks, Southern New York to Georgia.   Six to fifteen
inches high, with brown and shining stalks.

*Fronds.*—Oblong-lance-shaped, rough with rusty hairs, twice-
pinnate; *pinnæ* rather distant, triangular-ovate, cut into oblong,
more or less incised pinnules; *fruit-dots* roundish; *indusium*
formed by the reflexed margins of the lobes which are pushed back
by the matured sporangia.

Till a few years ago the most northern station for
the Hairy Lip Fern was supposed to be within the
limits of New York City.   The plant was discovered, in 1866 or 1867, on Manhattan Island, near Fort
Tryon, growing on rocks with an eastern exposure.
If one should visit this station to-day he would find
himself at 196th Street, in the city of New York,
some two hundred and thirty-three yards west of
the Kingsbridge road, and I fear there would be no
trace of this to us rare fern.

Since then the plant has been discovered close to
the Hudson River at Poughkeepsie.

Its narrowly oblong, dull-green fronds, more or
less covered with red-brown hairs, which give it a
somewhat rusty appearance, spring from the clefts
and ledges of rocks.

PLATE XIII

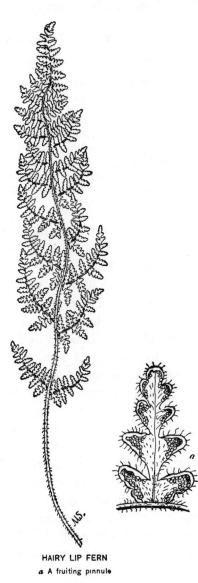

HAIRY LIP FERN

*a* A fruiting pinnule

## 23. HAY-SCENTED FERN

*Dicksonia pilosiuscula* (*D. punctilobula*)

Two to three feet high; hill-sides, meadows, and thickets from Canada to Tennessee.

*Fronds.*—Ovate-lance-shaped, long-tapering, pale-green, thin and very delicate in texture, slightly glandular and hairy, usually thrice-pinnatifid; *pinnæ* lance-shaped, pointed, repeating in miniature outline of frond; *pinnules* cut again into short and obtuse lobes or segments; *fruit-dots* each on an elevated globular receptacle on a *recurved toothlet; indusium* cup-shaped, open at the top.

In parts of the country, especially from Connecticut southward, the Hay-scented Fern is one of the abundant plants. Though not essentially a rock-loving plant, it rejoices in such rocky, upland pastures as crown many of our lower mountain ranges, "great stretches of grayish or sage-green fields in which every bowlder and outcrop of rock is marked by masses of the bright-green fronds of *Dicksonia*, over which the air moves lazily, heavy with the peculiar fragrance of this interesting fern." Its singularly delicate, tapering, pale-green fronds, curving gracefully in every direction, rank it among our most beautiful and noticeable ferns. Often along the roadsides it forms great masses of feathery foliage, tempting the weary pedestrian or bicycler to fling himself upon a couch sufficiently soft and luxurious in appearance to satisfy a sybarite. But I can testify that the Hay-scented Fern does not make so good a bed as it promises.

Two years ago, during a memorably hot August,

PLATE XIV

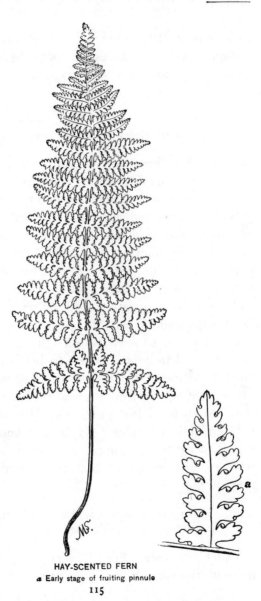

HAY-SCENTED FERN

*a* Early stage of fruiting pinnule

115

an afternoon drive over an unused mountain road brought us to a picturesque spot where the clear stream tumbled into a rock-paved basin, suggesting so vividly the joy of

" —— the cool silver shock
Of the plunge in a pool's living water,"

that then and there we resolved soon to pitch our tent upon its banks. In all respects it was not a suitable camp site. There were no balsams or ever-greens of any kind available for bedding in the neighborhood, so when, a few days later, we had taken up our quarters just above the rock-paved pool, we went into our temporary back-yard where the *Dicksonia* grew abundantly with its usual soft and seductive appearance, and gathered great arm-fuls for the night's rest. I must frankly own that I never slept on so hard a bed. Since then I have been more than ever inclined to believe that ferns inhabit the earth chiefly for decorative ends. In the present age they do not lend themselves as once they did to medicinal purposes. Usually they are without culinary value. So far as I know animals refuse to eat them on account of their acrid juices. And experience proves that when used as a bed they do not

" —— medicine thee to that sweet sleep
Which thou owedst yesterday."

The Hay-scented Fern is very sensitive, wither-ing with the early frosts. Sometimes in the fall it

116

bleaches almost white. Then its slender fronds seem like beautiful wraiths of their former selves.

The *Dicksonia*, as he always calls it, is Thoreau's favorite among the ferns. Its fronds are sweet-scented when crushed or in drying, and to their fragrance he was peculiarly sensitive:

"Going along this old Carlisle road . . . road where all wild things and fruits abound, where there are countless rocks to jar those who venture in wagons; road which leads to and through a great but not famous garden, zoölogical and botanical, at whose gate you never arrive—as I was going along there, I perceived the grateful scent of the Dicksonia fern now partly decayed. It reminds me of all up country, with its springy mountain-sides and unexhausted vigor. Is there any essence of Dicksonia fern, I wonder? Surely that giant, who my neighbor expects is to bound up the Alleghenies, will have his handkerchief scented with that. The sweet fragrance of decay! When I wade through by narrow cow-paths, it is as if I had strayed into an ancient and decayed herb garden. Nature perfumes her garments with this essence now especially. She gives it to those who go a-barberrying and on dark autumnal walks. The very scent of it, if you have a decayed frond in your chamber, will take you far up country in a twinkling. You would think you had gone after the cows there, or were lost on the mountains."

Again:

"Why can we not oftener refresh one another

with original thoughts ? If the fragrance of the
Dicksonia fern is so grateful and suggestive to us,
how much more refreshing and encouraging, recre-
ating, would be fresh and fragrant thoughts com-
municated to us from a man's experience ? I want
none of his pity nor sympathy in the common sense,
but that he should emit and communicate to me his
essential fragrance . . . going a-huckleberrying
in the fields of thought, and enriching all the world
with his vision and his joys."

In connection with this fern Thoreau indulges in
one of those whimsical, enchanting disquisitions
with the spirit of which you are in complete accord,
even though you may seem to contradict the letter :

" It is only when we forget all our learning that
we begin to know. I do not get nearer by a hair's-
breadth to any natural object, so long as I presume
that I have an introduction to it from some learned
man. To conceive of it with a total apprehension,
I must for the thousandth time approach it as something totally strange. If you would make acquaintance with the ferns, you must forget your botany.
Not a single scientific term or distinction is the
least to the purpose. You would fain perceive
something, and you must approach the object totally unprejudiced. You must be aware that nothing is what you have taken it to be. In what book
is this world and its beauty described ? Who has
plotted the steps toward the discovery of beauty ?
You must be in a different state from common.
Your greatest success will be simply to perceive

that such things are, and you will have no com-
munication to make to the Royal Society. If it
were required to know the position of the fruit-dots
or the character of the indusium, nothing could be
easier than to ascertain it; but if it is required that
you be affected by ferns, that they amount to anything, signify anything to you, that they be another
sacred scripture and revelation to you, helping to
redeem your life, this end is not so easily accomplished."

# GROUP V

## FERTILE AND STERILE FRONDS LEAF-LIKE AND SIMILAR ; SPORANGIA IN LINEAR OR OBLONG FRUIT-DOTS

### 24. LADY FERN

*Asplenium Filix-fœmina*

A wood and roadside fern, growing in all parts of the country
and presenting many varying forms.   One to three feet high,
with tufted, straw-colored, reddish, or brownish stalks.

*Fronds.*—Broadly lance-shaped, tapering toward the apex, twice-
pinnate ; *pinnæ* lance-shaped ; *pinnules* oblong-lanceolate, toothed
or incised ; *fruit-dots* short, curved ; *indusium* delicate, curved,
sometimes shaped like a horseshoe.

The Lady Fern is found in all parts of the country.  Sometimes it forms a part of the tangle of wild,
graceful things which grow close to the roadside
fence.   Again, in company with the Silvery Spleenwort, the Evergreen Wood Fern and the Spinulose
Shield Fern, forming perhaps a background for
the brilliant scarlet clusters of the wild bergamot,
it fringes the banks of some amber-colored brook
which surprises us with its swift, noiseless flow as
we stroll through the woods.

The earliest fronds uncurl in May.   In June the

PLATE XV

LADY FERN

*a* Fruiting pinnule          *b* Portion of same

121

plant is very graceful and pleasing. When growing in shaded places it is often conspicuous by reason of its bright pink or reddish stalks, which contrast effectively with the delicate green of the foliage. But in later summer, judging by my own experience, the Lady Fern loses much of its delicacy. Many of its fronds become disfigured and present a rather blotched and coarse appearance.

This seems strange in view of the fact that the plant is called by Lowe, a well-known English writer, the " Queen of Ferns," and that it is one of the few ferns to which we find reference in literature. Scott pays it the compliment, rarely bestowed upon ferns, of mentioning it by name:

> " Where the copse wood is the greenest,
> Where the fountain glistens sheenest,
> Where the morning dew lies longest,
> There the Lady Fern grows strongest."

In English works devoted to ferns I find at least two poems, more remarkable for enthusiasm than for poetic inspiration, in its honor. I quote a portion of the one which occurs in Miss Pratt's " Ferns of Great Britain and Their Allies ":

> " But seek her not in early May,
> For a Sibyl then she looks,
> With wrinkled fronds that seem to say,
> ' Shut up are my wizard books ! '
> Then search for her in the summer woods,
> Where rills keep moist the ground,
> Where Foxgloves from their spotted hoods,
> Shake pilfering insects round ;

When up and clambering all about,
　The Traveller's Joy flings forth
Its snowy awns, that in and out
　Like feathers strew the earth :
Fair are the tufts of meadow-sweet
　That haply blossom nigh ;
Fair are the whirls of violet
　Prunella shows hard by ;
But nor by burn in wood, or vale,
　Grows anything so fair
As the plumy crest of emerald pale,
That waves in the wind, and soughs in the gale,
Of the Lady Fern, when the sunbeams turn
　To gold her delicate hair."

The other, which I give in full, on account of its
quaintness, appeared in the *Botanical Looker-out* of
Edwin Lees :

" When in splendor and beauty all nature is crown'd,
　The Fern is seen curling half hid in the ground,
　But of all the green brackens that rise by the burn,
　Commend me alone to the sweet Lady Fern.

" Polypodium indented stands stiff on the rock,
　With his sori exposed to the tempest's rough shock ;
　On the wide, chilly heath Aquilina stands stern,
　Not once to be named with the sweet Lady Fern.

" Filix-mas in a circle lifts up his green fronds
　And the Heath Fern delights by the bogs and the ponds ;
　Through their shadowy tufts though with pleasure I turn,
　The palm must still rest with the fair Lady Fern.

" By the fountain I see her just spring into sight,
　Her texture as frail as though shivering with fright ;
　To the water she shrinks—I can scarcely discern
　In the deep humid shadows the soft Lady Fern.

123

" Where the water is pouring forever she sits,
And beside her the Ouzel, the Kingfisher flits ;
There, supreme in her beauty, beside the full urn,
In the shade of the rock stands the tall Lady Fern.

" Noon burns up the mountain ; but here by the fall
The Lady Fern flourishes graceful and tall.
Hours speed as thoughts rise, without any concern,
And float like the spray gliding past the green Fern."

### 25. SILVERY SPLEENWORT

*Asplenium thelypteroides* (*A. acrostichoides*)

Entire frond

Canada to Alabama and westward, in rich woods.   One to three feet high.

*Fronds.* — Lance-shaped, tapering both ways from the middle, once-pinnate; *pinnæ* linear-lanceolate, deeply cut into obtuse segments ; *fruit-dots* oblong; *indusium* silvery when young.

The Silvery Spleenwort grows in company with its kinsman, the Narrow-leaved Spleenwort, and also with many of the Aspidiums, such as the Spinulose Shield Fern, the Evergreen Wood Fern, the Christmas and Goldie's Fern.   I find it growing in large patches in the rich woods, often near water, either in boggy ground or on the very edge of the clear, brown brook. Sometimes it is difficult to detect a single fertile frond in a group of plants covering many square feet of ground.   This is probably owing

124

PLATE XVI

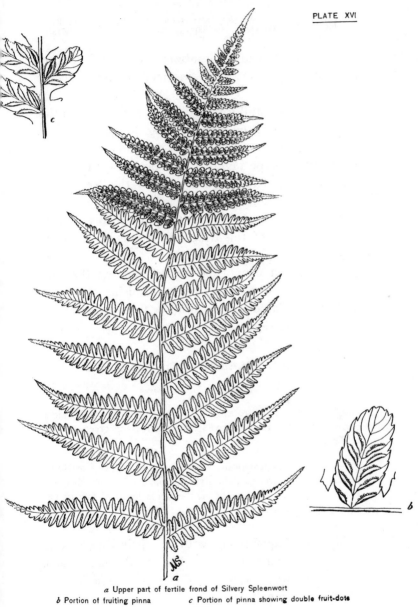

*a* Upper part of fertile frond of Silvery Spleenwort
*b* Portion of fruiting pinna          *c* Portion of pinna showing double fruit-dots

125

to the deeply shaded situations which it favors, as in sunny exposures I have noticed an abundance of fertile fronds.

Its color is a dull green, the silvery indusia on the lower surfaces of the pinnæ giving the plant its English title. Although usually its fronds are larger, their outline, tapering as it does both ways from the middle, somewhat suggests that of the New York Fern. It is readily identified, as the oblong or linear fruit-dots at once proclaim it a Spleenwort, and no other member of this tribe has fronds of the same shape.

Although it cannot be classed among the rare ferns, it is absent from many promising localities, and is associated in my mind with especially successful expeditions.

### 26. RUE SPLEENWORT. WALL RUE

*Asplenium Ruta-muraria*

A small rock fern, growing on limestone, Vermont to Michigan and southward. Four to seven inches long, with green, slender, tufted stalks.

*Fronds.*—Triangular-ovate, smooth, evergreen, twice or thrice-pinnate below; *pinnæ* cut into stalked pinnules; *fruit-dots* confluent at maturity, covering nearly the whole lower surface of pinnules; *indusium* delicate.

My first acquaintance with the little Rue Spleenwort in its own home dates back to the memorable day when we discovered the new station for the Hart's Tongue.

126

PLATE XVII

RUE SPLEENWORT

As I have already mentioned in my description of the Purple Cliff Brake, on a chance morning call I learned that twenty-five years before the Rue Spleenwort and the Purple Cliff Brake had been found on certain cliffs which overhung some neighboring falls.

On these very cliffs a quarter of a century later we found a few specimens of each plant. The tiny fronds of the Rue Spleenwort grew from small fissures in the cliffs, flattening themselves against their rocky background.

About a month later we returned to the spot for the purpose of securing photographs of the natural gallery where the plants grew. The seamed, overhanging rocks, the neighboring stream plunging nearly two hundred feet to the ravine below, the bold opposite cliffs showing here and there through their cloak of trees, and above and beyond the smiling upland pastures, the wood-crowned hills, and the haze-softened valley, had left a picture in the mind that we hoped to reproduce, however inadequately, by means of the camera.

This morning we had approached the cliffs from an opposite direction. In climbing a gradual ascent from the bed of the stream, we found a plant of the Rue Spleenwort which was more vigorous and thrifty than any we had previously seen. In the single tuft, about as large as the palm of one's hand, we counted forty-five green fronds. Their lower surfaces, in many cases, were covered with confluent fruit-dots. The plant had much the effect of a rather small specimen of the Mountain Spleenwort. The short, broad fronds were somewhat leathery, with only a few pinnæ. Considering its lack of size, the little cluster, springing from the bare rock, made so definite and interesting a picture that we tried to photograph it as it grew. But after some time spent in striving to secure a foothold for the tripod, and at the same time for the photographer, we gave up the attempt as hopeless.

In England the Rue Spleenwort is found growing on old walls, specially on their northern sides, also on church-towers, bridges, and ruins. It is said to be difficult to cultivate.

Formerly this fern yielded a decoction which was supposed to be beneficial in attacks of pleurisy and of jaundice.

## 27. MOUNTAIN SPLEENWORT

*Asplenium montanum*

Connecticut and New York to Georgia. A small rock fern from two to eight inches long, with stalks brown at base.

*Fronds.* — Ovate-lanceolate in outline, somewhat leathery, cut into oblong pinnæ, the lower ones of which are cut again into more or less oblong, toothed divisions, the upper ones less and less divided; *rachis* green, broad, flat; *fruit-dots* linear, short; *indusium* thin, hidden at length by the sporangia, which mature in July.

With us this plant is decidedly rare. New York and Connecticut are given as its northern limits. I have found it only in one locality, in the neighborhood of a mountain lake in Ulster County, N. Y. Though growing here somewhat abundantly, the fern is so small that, unless your eyes are trained to search every cranny in the hope of some new find, you are not likely to notice it. Even with trained eyes you may readily fancy that the narrow chinks in the cliffs which rise sheerly from the lake are merely patched with moss. But when you have pulled your boat close under the shelving rocks,

PLATE XVIII

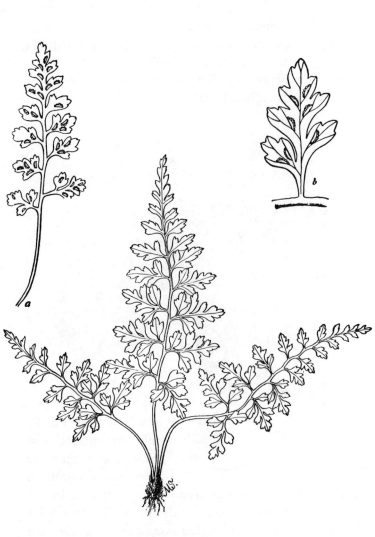

**MOUNTAIN SPLEENWORT**

*a* A fertile frond          *b* A pinna of fertile frond

and have secured a hold that enables you to stand up and examine at leisure the suspicious patches, your heart bounds with delight as you get a near view of the fringe of blue-green, leathery fronds which flatten themselves against the gray

Mountain Spleenwort

cliffs. Apparently only the plants that grow under specially favorable conditions are able to develop fronds that attain a length of five or six inches. Only in what must have been almost constant shadow, under the shelving rocks, directly above the lake and refreshed always by its moisture, did I find these really attractive, thrifty-looking plants. The specimens, which were located at some distance from the lake, growing in one instance on top of a mountain, again in the shaded crevices of a cliff, were tiny, indefinite-looking plants with nothing to recommend them to any eyes save those of the fern collector. In every instance they grew from fissures in the rocks, rooting apparently in a mere pinch of earth, yet with such tenacity that it would have been very difficult to extract a plant unharmed. In almost every case they were shielded much of the time from exposure to the sun.

The large plants in the immediate vicinity of the lake were noticeably bluish-green in color.

It is to be hoped that the few known haunts of the Mountain Spleenwort will be respected in order that this rare little plant may be preserved.

## 28. EBONY SPLEENWORT

*Asplenium ebeneum (A. platyneuron)*

Maine to Florida and westward, on rocks and hill-sides. Nine to eighteen inches high, with blackish and shining stalks.

*Fronds.*—Upright, narrowly oblanceolate, fertile fronds much the taller, once-pinnate; *pinnæ* usually alternate, oblong, finely toothed, the base auricled on the upper or on both sides; *fruit-dots* many, oblong, nearer midvein than margin; *indusium* silvery till maturity.

The slender fronds of the Ebony Spleenwort hold themselves with a sort of rigid grace which suggests

Portion of fertile frond

a combination of delicacy and endurance.

It is an attractive plant with an elusiveness of habit which serves, perhaps, to increase its charm. Its range is from Maine to Florida and westward; it is said to prefer limestone soil, and my past experience has proved it a fairly common plant, yet so far this summer, in many expeditions in a part of the country rich in limestone, I have found only one specimen, while last year along the roadsides of Long Island I found its black-stemmed fronds standing erect and slim in crowded ranks under groups of red cedars. In other years it has abounded in localities of a different character,

Fertile pinna magnified

sometimes following its little relative, the Maidenhair Spleenwort, into moist ravines or along

PLATE XIX

EBONY SPLEENWORT

the shelves of shaded rocks, again climbing exposed hill-sides, where its fresh beauty is always a surprise.

The fronds of the Ebony Spleenwort usually face the sun, even if so doing necessitates the twisting of its stalk.

### 29. MAIDENHAIR SPLEENWORT

*Asplenium Trichomanes*

Almost throughout North America.   A small rock fern, four to twelve inches long, with purplish-brown and shining, thread-like stalks.

*Fronds.*—Linear in outline, somewhat rigid, once-pinnate; *pinnæ* roundish or oval, unequal-sided, attached to rachis by a narrow point, entire or toothed; *fruit-dots* short, oblong, narrowed at the ends, three to six on each side of the midrib; *sporangia* dark-brown when ripe; *indusium* delicate.

In childhood the delicate little fronds and dark, glistening, thread-like stalks of the Maidenhair Spleenwort seemed to me a token of the mysterious,

Fertile pinnæ

ecstatic presence of the deeper woods, of woods where dark hemlocks arched across the rock-broken stream, where the spongy ground was carpeted with low, nameless plants with white-veined or shining leaves and coral-like berries, where precious red-cupped mosses covered the fallen tree-trunks and strange birds sang unknown songs.

Perhaps because in those days it was a rare plant

to be met with on rare occasions, in a spirit of
breathless exultation, I almost begrudge finding it
now on shaded cliffs close to the highway.

Certainly it seems lovelier when it holds itself
somewhat aloof from the beaten paths.   One of its
favorite   haunts   is   a
mossy cliff which forms

part of a ra-
vine of sin-
g u l a r
beauty.
A l o n g
the base
of   this
cliff f o a m s
a r u s h i n g
stream on its way
to the valley. Over-
head stretch branches of hem-
lock,  cedar,  and  basswood.

Maidenhair Spleenwort

On the broader shelves the mountain maple, the
silver  birch,  and  the  hobble-bush  secure  a  pre-
carious foothold.   Below rare sunbeams bring out
rich  patches  of  color  on  the  smooth,  muscular
trunks  of  the  beeches.   Close  to  the  water,  perhaps,  wheel  a  pair  of  spotted  sand-pipers,  now

lighting on the rocks in order to secure some in-
sect, now tilting backward and forward with the

comical motion peculiar to them,
now gliding swiftly along the
pebbly shore till their brown and
gray and white coats are lost in
the brown and gray and white of

Lower pinnæ      shore, rock, and water.

In such a retreat as this ravine the Maidenhair
Spleenwort seems peculiarly at home.   Its tufted
fronds have a fresh greenness that
is a delight to the eye as they spring
from little pockets or crannies too
shallow, we would suppose, for the
necessary moisture and nourishment.
Its near companions are the Walking Fern, whose tapering, leaf-like,
blue-green fronds leap along the
shelving ledge above, and the Bulblet Bladder Fern,
which seems to gush from every crevice of the cliff.

Upper pinnæ

### 30. GREEN SPLEENWORT

*Asplenium viride*

Northern New England, west and northward, on shaded rocks.
A few inches to nearly a foot long, with tufted stalks, brownish
below, green above.

*Fronds.*—Linear-lanceolate, once-pinnate, pale green ; *pinnæ*
ovate, toothed, midvein indistinct and forking ; *fruit-dots* oblong ;
*indusium* straight or curved.

The Green Spleenwort in general appearance
resembles the Maidenhair Spleenwort.   Perhaps

138

PLATE XX

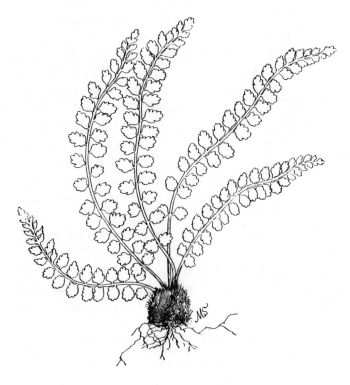

GREEN SPLEENWORT

its most distinguishing feature is its stalk, which,
though brown below, becomes green above, while
that of its little relative is dark and shining throughout.  Its discovery on Mt. Mansfield, Vt., by Mr.
Pringle gave it a place in the flora of the United

States, as is shown in the
following passage from Mr
Pringle's address before the
Vermont Botanical Club:

"On this first visit to Mt.
Mansfield my work was re-
stricted to the crest of the
great mountain.  About the
cool and shaded cliffs in front
of the Summit House were
then first brought to my view

**Fertile pinnæ**

*Aspidium fragrans* . . . and
*Asplenium viride*, . . . for I was still on my fern
hunt.  The finding of the former added a species
to the Vermont catalogue; the latter was an addition to the flora of the United States.  Such little
discoveries gave joy to the young collector."

### 31. SCOTT'S SPLEENWORT

*Asplenium ebenoides*

Connecticut to the Mississippi and southward to Alabama, on
limestone.  Four to twelve inches long, with blackish and
shining stalks.

*Fronds.*—Lanceolate, tapering to a long, narrow apex, generally
pinnate below, pinnatifid above; *fruit-dots* straight or slightly
curved; *indusium* narrow.

PLATE XXI

SCOTT'S SPLEENWORT

The known stations of this curious little plant are usually in the immediate neighborhood of the Walking Leaf and the Ebony Spleenwort, of which ferns it is supposed to be a hybrid.   The long, narrow apex occasionally forming a new plant, and the irregular fruit-dots remind one of the  Walking Leaf, while the lustrous black stalk, the free veins, and the pinnate portions of the fronds suggest the Ebony Spleenwort.

Scott's Spleenwort matures in August.   It is rare and local, except in Alabama.   The fact, however, that it has been discovered in widely distant localities east of the Mississippi should lend excitement to fern expeditions in any of our limestone neighborhoods where we see its  chosen associates, the Walking Leaf and the Ebony Spleenwort.   To find a new station for this interesting little fern, even if it consisted of one or two plants only, as is said to have been the case at Canaan, Conn., would well repay the fatigue of the longest tramp.

### 32. PINNATIFID SPLEENWORT

*Asplenium pinnatifidum*

New Jersey and Pennsylvania to Illinois, and southward to Alabama and Arkansas, on rocks.   Four to fourteen inches long, with polished stalks, blackish below, green above, when young somewhat chaffy below.

*Fronds.*—Broadly lance-shaped, tapering to a long, slender point, pinnatifid or pinnate below ; *pinnæ* rounded or the lowest tapering to a point , *fruit-dots* straight or somewhat curved ; *indusium* straight or curved.

PLATE XXII

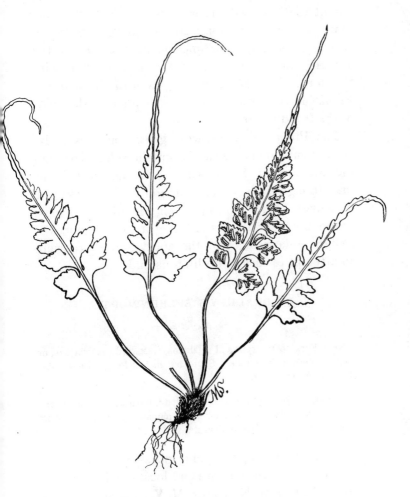

PINNATIFID SPLEENWORT

143

This plant resembles the Walking Leaf to such an extent that formerly it was not considered a separate species. The long, slender apex of its frond, which, it is said, sometimes takes root, as in the Walking Leaf, gave ground for its confusion with that fern. But the tapering apex of the frond of the Pinnàtifid Spleenwort is not so long and the veins of the frond are free.

The Pinnatifid Spleenwort grows on rocks. Its usual companions are the Mountain Spleenwort and the Maidenhair Spleenwort. Williamson tells us that, though it is quite common in Kentucky, he has never found a frond which rooted at the apex. Eaton, however, speaks of "one or two instances of a slight enlargement of the apex, as if there were an attempt to form a proliferous bud."

### 33. BRADLEY'S SPLEENWORT

*Asplenium Bradleyi*

New York to Georgia and Alabama, westward to Arkansas, on rocks preferring limestone. Six to ten inches long, with slender, chestnut-brown stalks.

*Fronds.*—Oblong-lanceolate or oblong, tapering to a point, pinnate; *pinnæ* oblong-ovate, lobed or pinnatifid; *fruit-dots* short, near the midrib; *indusium* delicate.

To my knowledge the only place in the northeastern States where this rare and local species has been collected is near Newburg, N. Y., where Dr. Eaton found a plant growing on lime rock in 1864.

PLATE XXIII

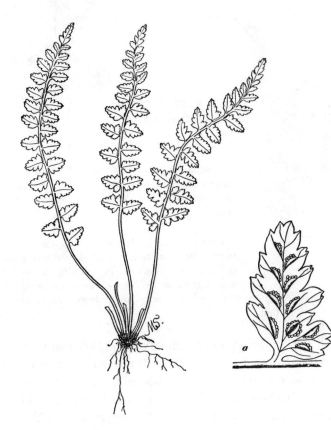

BRADLEY S SPLEENWORT

*a* Fertile pinna

145

### 34. WALKING FERN.
### WALKING LEAF

*Camptosorus rhizophyllus*

Canada to North Carolina and westward, on shaded rocks, preferring limestone. Four to eighteen inches long, with light-green stalks.

*Fronds.*—Simple, lanceolate, long-tapering toward the apex, usually heart-shaped at base, the apex often rooting and forming a new plant ; *fruit-dots* oblong or linear, irregularly scattered on the lower surface of the frond ; *indusium* thin.

To its unusual and suggestive title this plant undoubtedly owes much of the interest which it seems to arouse in the minds of those who do not profess to be fern-lovers. A friend tells me that as a child, eagerly on the lookout for this apparently active little plant, he was so much influenced by its title that he thought it might be advantageous to secure a butterfly-net as an aid in its capture. I find that older people as well are tempted to unwonted energy if promised a glimpse of the Walking Fern. Then,

146

too, the scarcity of the plant in many localities, or,
indeed, its entire absence from certain parts of the
country, gives it a reputation for rarity which is one
of the most certain roads to fame.

For many years I was unable to track it to any of
its haunts. During a summer spent in Rensselaer
County, N. Y., the Walking Leaf was the object of
various expeditions. I recall one drive of twenty-
five miles devoted to hunting up a rumored station.
At the end of the day, which
turned out cold and rainy, and
fruitless so far as its special object was concerned, I felt inclined to believe that the plant
had justified its title and had
walked out of the neighborhood.
Yet, after all, no such expedition, even with wind and weather
against one, as in this case, is
really fruitless. The sharp watch
along the roadside, the many
little expeditions into inviting

Portion of fertile frond

pastures, up promising cliffs, over moss-grown bowld-
ers, down to the rocky border of the brook, are sure
to result in discoveries of value or in moments of
delight. A flower yet unnamed, a butterfly beautiful
as a gem, an unfamiliar bird-song traced to its source,
a new, suggestive outlook over the well-known valley, and, later, "a sleep pleasant with all the influences
of long hours in the open air "—any or all of these
results may be ours, and go to make the day count.

147

Finally, one September afternoon, shortly before leaving the neighborhood, we resolved upon a last search, in quite a new direction. Several miles from home, at a fork in the road, standing in a partially wooded pasture, we noticed just such a large, shaded rock, with mossy ledges, as had filled us with vain hopes many times. J. suggested a closer examination, which I discouraged, remembering previous disappointments. But something in the look of the great bowlder provoked his curiosity, so over the fence and up the ledges he scrambled. Almost his first resting-place was a projecting shelf which was carpeted with a mat of bluish-green foliage. It needed only a moment's investigation to identify the leathery, tapering fronds of the Walking Fern. No one who has not spent hours in some such search as this can sympathize with the delight of those moments. We fairly gloated over the quaint little plants, following with our fingers the slender tips of the fronds till they rooted in the moss, starting another generation on its life journey, and earning for itself the title of Walking Leaf or Walking Fern.

Although since then I have found the Walking Leaf frequently, and in great abundance, I do not remember ever to have seen it make so fine a display. The plants were unusually large and vigorous, and the aspect of the matted tufts was uncommonly luxuriant. To be sure, some allowance must be made for the glamour of a first meeting.

The Walking Leaf grows usually on limestone

rocks, though it has been found on sandstone, shale, and conglomerate as well. I have also seen it on the stumps of decaying trees near limestone cliffs in Central New York, where it is a common plant, creeping along the shaded, mossy ledges above star-like tufts of the Maidenhair Spleenwort and fragile clusters of the Slender Cliff Brake, venturing to the brook's edge with sprays of the Bulblet Bladder Fern, and climbing the turreted summits of the hills close to the Purple Cliff Brake.

Although without the grace of the Maidenhair, the delicacy of certain of the Spleenworts, or the stately beauty of the Shield Ferns, the oddity and sturdiness of this little plant are bound to make it a favorite everywhere.

Occasionally a plant is found which will keep up its connection with two or three generations; that is, a frond will root at the apex, forming a new plant (the second generation). This will also send out a rooting frond which gives birth to a new plant (the third generation) before the two first fronds have decayed at their tips so as to sever the connection.

At times forking fronds are found, these forks also rooting occasionally at their tips.

## 35. HART'S TONGUE

*Scolopendrium vulgare* (*S. scolopendrium*)

Shaded ravines under limestone cliffs in Central New York and near South Pittsburg, Tenn.   A few inches to nearly two feet long, with stalks which are chaffy below and sometimes to the base of the leaf.

*Fronds.*—Narrowly oblong, undivided, from a somewhat heart-shaped base, bright-green ; *fruit-dots* linear, elongated, a row on either side of the midrib and at right angles to it ; *indusium* appearing to be double.

When Gray describes a fern as "very rare" and Dr. Britton limits it to two small stations in neighboring counties in the whole northern United States, the fern lover looks forward with a sense of eager anticipation to seeing it for the first time.

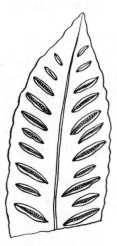

Tip of fertile frond

During a week spent at Cazenovia, N. Y., a few years ago, I learned that the rare Hart's Tongue grew at Chittenango Falls, only four miles away. But my time was limited, and on a single brief visit to the picturesque spot where the broad Chittenango stream dashes over cliffs one hundred and fifty feet high, losing itself in the wild, wooded glen below on its journey to the distant valley, I did little more than revel in the beauty of the foaming mass which for many days " haunted me like a pas-

sion." I saw no signs of the plant which has done almost as much as "the sounding cataract" to make the spot famous.

The combined recollection of the beautiful falls and the for me undiscovered fern, joined to the fact that Madison and the adjoining Onondaga County are favorite hunting grounds for the fern lover on account of the many species which they harbor, drew us to Cazenovia for the summer two years later.

Guided by the explicit directions of Mr. J. H. Ten Eyck Burr, a fern enthusiast who is always ready to share with others, of whose good faith he is assured, his enjoyment of the hiding-places of his favorites, we found at last the Hart's Tongue in its own home.

Hart's Tongue

If Mr. Burr's kindness in sending me some fine pressed specimens, and the illustrations I had seen in various books, had not already made me familiar with the general look of the plant, the long, undivided, tongue-like fronds, so different from one's preconceived notion of a fern, would have been a great surprise. Even now, although I have visited many times its hidden retreats, and have noted with delight every detail of its glossy, vigorous growth, it seems to me always as rare and unusual as it did the first day I found it.

At Chittenango Falls the Hart's Tongue grows a few yards from the base of bold, overhanging limestone cliffs, the tops of which are fringed by pendent roots of the red cedar. Nearly always it is caught beneath moss-grown fragments of the fallen limestone, the bright-green, undulating, glossy leaves either standing almost erect (curving outward slightly above) or else falling over toward the slope of the land so as to present a nearly prostrate appearance. At times these fronds are very numerous, as many as fifty to a plant, forming great clumps of foliage. Again we find a plant with only half a dozen or even fewer green fronds. At maturity the linear, bright-brown fruit-dots, a row on either side the midrib, are conspicuous on the lower surfaces of the fronds.

This haunt of the Hart's Tongue is shaded by a growth of tall basswoods and maples, of sturdy oaks and hemlocks. The neighboring cliffs are draped with the slender fronds of the Bulblet Blad-

der Fern. On every side rise the tall crowns of the
omnipresent Evergreen Wood Fern. Lower down,
close to the rushing stream which we see mistily
through the green branches, its roar always in our
ears, grow the Walking Leaf and the Maidenhair.
The little Polypody climbs over the rocks and
perches contentedly on the spreading roots of trees,
while a few fragile plants of the Slender Cliff Brake,
something of a rarity in these parts, are fastened to
the mossy ledges.

The other published northern station of the
Hart's Tongue is at Jamesville, some fifteen miles
from Chittenango Falls, near a small sheet of water
known commonly as Green Pond, christened botan-
ically Scolopendrium Lake. Here also it grows
among the talus at the foot of limestone cliffs. The
plants which I found in this locality were less luxuriant than those at Chittenango Falls. They grow
in more exposed, less shaded spots.

Scolopendrium Lake has become somewhat famous in the world of fern students by reason of
Mr. Underwood's claim that in its immediate vicinity, within a radius of fifty rods from the water's
edge (the lake being a mere pond), grow twenty-
seven different kinds of ferns, while within a circle
whose diameter is not over three miles thirty-four
species have been found. During this one day we
gave to the neighborhood, we could not hope to
find so great a number, the result, perhaps, of many
days' investigation, and were forced to content ourselves with the twenty-one species we did find. In

his list Mr. Underwood marks the Purple Cliff
Brake as found but once, so I judge he did not discover the station on the turreted cliffs close by
where it grows in extravagant profusion, producing
fronds not only much longer and finer than I had
seen elsewhere, but superior to those pictured in
the illustrated books.

During the same summer, on an expedition to
Perryville Falls, which we had planned for the
express purpose of finding the Rue Spleenwort and
the Purple Cliff Brake, a new station was discovered for the Hart's Tongue. To Miss Murray Ledyard, of Cazenovia, belongs the honor of finding the
first plants in this locality. We had been successful in the original object of our journey, and had
crossed the stream in order to examine the opposite cliffs. J. and I, curious to study the wet wall
of rock close to the sheer white veil of water, which
fell more than one hundred feet, finally secured
an unsubstantial foothold among graceful tufts of
the greenish, lily-like flowers, which ought to receive a more homely and appropriate title than
*Zygadenus elegans.* Having satisfied ourselves that
the mossy crevices harbored no plants of the Slender Cliff Brake, now the immediate object of our
search, we followed the natural path beneath the
overhanging rock and above the sheer descent to
the ravine, examining the cliffs as we cautiously
picked our way. Miss Ledyard had remained below, and suddenly we heard her give a triumphant
shout, followed by the joyful announcement that

she had found the Hart's Tongue. The station being previously quite unknown, this was a most interesting discovery. On entering the ravine we had discussed its possibility, but I had fancied that any hope of it would be unfounded, as I supposed the ground had been thoroughly canvassed by the many botanists who had visited the neighborhood.

The plants were still young, but large and vigorous, growing in a partial opening among the basswoods, maples, and beeches, on a steep slope covered with fragments of limestone, some thirty or forty feet from the base of the cliffs. We must have found from twenty to thirty plants within a radius of as many feet.

Unfortunately, as it turned out, the discovery found its way to the columns of the local paper, and on our return to the station, some weeks later our eager expectation of seeing the young plants in the splendor of maturity was crushed by finding that the spot had been ruthlessly invaded and a number of the finest plants had disappeared. Before long it will be necessary for botanists to form a secret society, with vows of silence as to fern localities and some sort of lynch law for the punishment of vandals.

This fern, so rare with us, is a common plant in Europe, its fronds attaining at times a length of two or three feet. In Ireland and the Channel Islands it is especially abundant. In Devonshire, England, it is described as growing " on the tops and at the sides of walls ; hanging from old ruins . . . drop-

ping down its long, green fronds into the cool
and limpid water of roadside wells hewn out of the
rock ; often exposed to the full blaze of the sun,
but always in such cases dwindled down to a tiny
size " (" The Fern Paradise ").

The Hart's Tongue has been known as the Cater-
pillar Fern and the Seaweed Fern.

### 36. VIRGINIA CHAIN FERN

*Woodwardia Virginica*

Swampy places, often in deep water, from Maine to Florida. Two
to more than three feet high.

*Fronds.*—Once-pinnate ; *pinnæ* pinnatifid, with oblong segments ; *fruit-dots* oblong, in chain-like rows along the midrib
both of the pinnæ and of the lobes, confluent when ripe ; *indusium*
fixed by its outer margin, opening on the side next the midrib.

Emerging from the shade and silence of a little
wood upon the rolling downs where one has
glimpses of the blue bay, our attention is attracted
by a tall fern beside the path, growing among a
tangle of shrubs and vines. It does not grow in
symmetrical crowns or tufts like an *Osmunda*, but
its fronds are almost as handsome, the divisions
being wider apart and more scattered. Turning
over two or three of the rather glossy fronds, we
find a rusty-backed, fertile frond, covered on one
side with the regular chain-like rows of fruit-dots
which make its name of Chain Fern seem very
appropriate and descriptive.

156

PLATE XXIV

UPPER PART OF FROND OF VIRGINIA CHAIN FERN
*a* Portion of fertile pinna          *b* Tip of fertile pinna

157

In the low, damp ground near the coast one may
expect to find this fern ; its haunts, where the narrow path winds between tall masses of sweet-pepper
bush and wet meadows where pogonia and calopo-
gon delight us in July, and the white-fringed orchids
may be found in later summer, are among the most
beautiful of the many beautiful kinds of country
that the fern and flower lover knows, to which his
feet stray inevitably in the season of green things,
and which are the solace of his "inward eye" when
that season is past.

# GROUP VI

FERTILE AND STERILE FRONDS LEAF-LIKE AND USUALLY
SIMILAR, FRUIT-DOTS ROUND

## 37. NEW YORK FERN

*Aspidium Noveboracense* (*Dryopteris Noveboracensis*)

Newfoundland to South Carolina, in woods and open meadows. One to more than two feet high, with stalks shorter than the
fronds.

*Fronds.* — Lance-shaped, tapering both ways from the middle
pinnate ; *pinnæ* lance-shaped, the lowest pairs shorter and deflexed,
divided into flat, oblong lobes which are not reflexed over the fruit-
dots ; *fruit-dots* round, distinct, near the margin ; *indusium* minute.

At times the pale-green fronds of the New York
Fern throng to the roadside, which is flanked by a
tangled thicket of Osmundas, wild roses, and elder
bushes.

Again, they stay quietly at home in the open marsh
or in the shadow of the hemlocks and cedars, where

159

they have fragrant pyrola and pipsissewa for company, and where the long, melancholy note of the
peewee breaks the silence.

This plant is easily distinguished from the Marsh
Fern by the noticeable tapering at both ends of its
frond, and by the flat instead of reflexed margins to
the lobes of the fertile pinnæ.

### 38. MARSH FERN

*Aspidium Thelypteris* (*Dryopteris Thelypteris*)

New Brunswick to Florida, in wet woods and swamps.    One to
nearly three feet high.

*Fronds.* — Lance-shaped, slightly downy, once-pinnate, fertile
fronds longer-stalked than the sterile; *pinnæ*, the lower ones hardly
smaller than the others, cut into oblong, entire lobes, which are obtuse in the sterile fronds, but appear acute in the fertile ones from
the strongly revolute margins; veins once or twice forked; *fruit-
dots* small, round, half-way between midvein and margin, or nearer
margin, soon confluent; *indusium* small.

In our wet woods and open swamps, and occasionally in dry pastures, the erect, fresh-green fronds of
the Marsh Fern grow abundantly.    The lowest pinnæ are set so high on the long slender stem as to
give the fern the appearance of trying to keep dry,
daintily holding its skirts out of the mud as it were.

The plant's range is wide.    As I pick my way
through marshy inland woods, using as bridges the
fallen trunks and interlacing roots of trees, its bright
fronds standing nearly three feet high, crowd about
me.    Close by, securing, like myself, a firmer foothold by the aid of the trees' roots, I notice the flat,

PLATE XXV

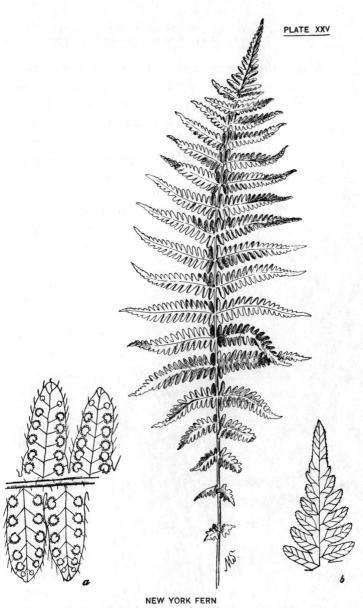

**NEW YORK FERN**

*a* Portion of fertile pinna          *b* Tip of pinna showing veining

mottled green and white rosettes and the
slender wands of flowers of the rattlesnake
orchid. In the open swamps beyond the
fern's companion is another
orchid, the ladies' tresses,
with braided spikes of white,
and in this case deliciously
fragrant flowers.

In open marshes near the
sea I find this plant associat-
ing itself with
the violet-
scented ad-
der's mouth,
with glis-
tening
sundew,
and with
gaudy
Turk's-
cap lilies.
From
the New

York Fern
it may be
distinguish-
ed easily by
the some-
what abrupt

Marsh Fern

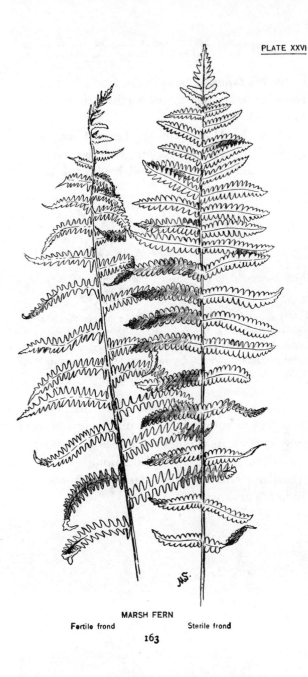

PLATE XXVI

MARSH FERN

Fertile frond       Sterile frond

163

instead of tapering base of the frond, by the strongly revolute margins of the fertile frond, and by its long stalk.

From the Massachusetts Fern it may be distinguished by its forked veins, the less revolute margins of the fertile frond, and by its thicker texture and deeper green.

### 39. MASSACHUSETTS FERN

*Aspidium simulatum (Dryopteris simulata)*

New Hampshire to the Indian Territory, in wooded swamps. One to more than three feet high.

*Fronds.*—Oblong-lance-shaped, little or not at all narrowed at the base, rather thin, pinnate ; *pinnæ* lance-shaped, cut into oblong, obtuse segments, which are slightly reflexed in the fertile fronds, veins not forked ; *fruit-dots* rather large, somewhat distant ; *indusium* " withering-persistent."

This species closely resembles the Marsh Fern. The less revolute margins of the fertile frond, the simple veins, its thinner texture, and its more distant fruit-dots aid in its identification. It is found in woodland swamps from New Hampshire to the Indian Territory.

PLATE XXVII

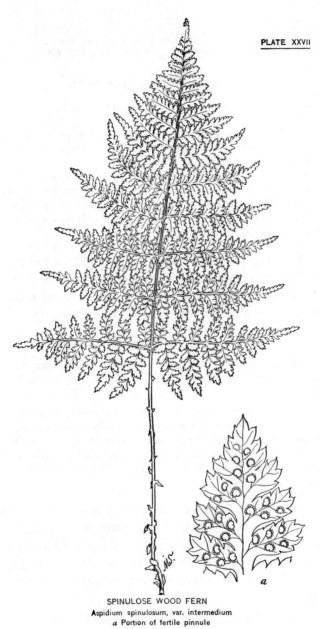

SPINULOSE WOOD FERN
Aspidium spinulosum, var. intermedium
*a* Portion of fertile pinnule

165

## 40. SPINULOSE WOOD FERN

*Aspidium spinulosum* (*Dryopteris spinulosa*)

Newfoundland to Kentucky.   The common European type, rare in North America.   One to two and a half feet high, with stalks having a few pale-brown deciduous scales.

*Fronds.*—Lance-ovate, twice-pinnate; *pinnæ* oblique to the rachis, elongated-triangular, the lower ones broadly triangular ; *pinnules* oblique to the midrib, connected by a narrow wing, cut into thorny-toothed segments; *fruit-dots* round ; *indusium* smooth, without marginal glands, soon withering.

To my knowledge I have only seen this fern in the herbarium, it being rare in this country.   It is found, I have been told, chiefly toward the tops of mountains.   Its pinnæ are noticeably ascending.

### Var. intermedium (D. spinulosa intermedia)

Labrador to North Carolina, in woods almost everywhere. Usually large, with somewhat chaffy stalks, having brown, dark-centred scales.

*Fronds.*—Oblong-ovate, 2-3 pinnate ; *pinnæ* oblong-lance-shaped, spreading, rather distant, the lowest unequally triangular, the pinnules on the lower side longer than those on the upper side ; *pinnules* ovate-oblong, spreading, with oblong lobes thorny-toothed at the apex ; *fruit-dots* round ; *indusium* delicate, beset with tiny stalked glands.

This is the form of the species that abounds in our woods.   Perhaps no one plant does more for their beauty than this stately fern, whose rich-green, outward-curving fronds spring in circles from fallen trees and decaying stumps as well as from the ground.

The plant varies greatly in height, breadth, and

PLATE XXVIII

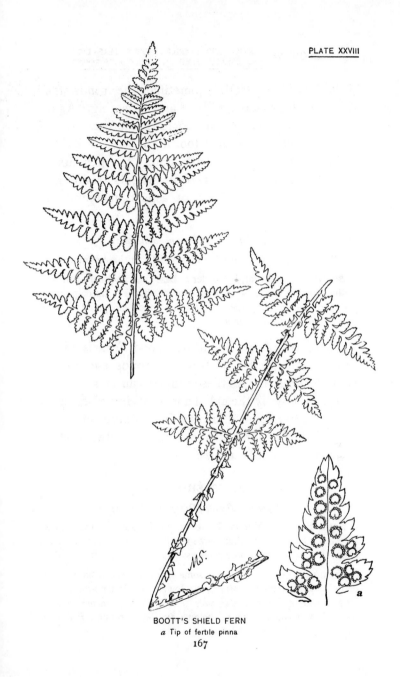

BOOT'S SHIELD FERN
*a* Tip of fertile pinna
167

way of holding itself.   Sometimes the fronds stand
three feet high, and are broad and spreading.   Again,
they are tall, slender, and somewhat erect.   Again,
they are not more than a foot high.

At its best it grows with almost tropical luxuriance and is a plant of rare beauty, its fronds having a certain featheriness of aspect uncommon in
the Aspidiums.

### Var. *dilatatum* (*D. spinulosa dilatata*)

Newfoundland to North Carolina, chiefly in the mountains.

*Fronds.*—Usually large, broader at base than in either of the preceding species, ovate or triangular-ovate, oftenest thrice-pinnate ;
*pinnules* lance-oblong, the lowest often much elongated ; *fruit-
dots* round ; *indusium* smooth.

This form of the Spinulose Wood Fern is distinguished chiefly by its broader fronds and by the
smooth indusia.   As these indusia can be seen satisfactorily only by the aid of a magnifying-glass, there
is frequently some difficulty in distinguishing this
variety.   Occasionally it occurs in a dwarf state,
fruiting when only a few inches high.

### 41. BOOTT'S SHIELD FERN

#### *Aspidium Boottii* (*Dryopteris Boottii*)

Nova Scotia to Maryland, about ponds and in wet places.
One and a half to more than three feet high, with somewhat chaffy
stalks which have pale-brown scales.

*Fronds.*—Long lance-shaped, somewhat narrowed at base, nearly
or quite twice-pinnate ; *pinnæ*, the lowest triangular-ovate, upper
longer and narrower ; *pinnules* oblong-ovate, sharply thorny-
toothed, somewhat pinnatifid below ; *fruit-dots* round ; *indusium*
slightly glandular.

PLATE XXIX

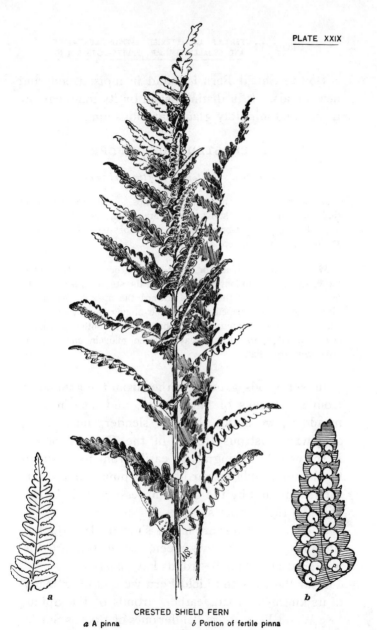

CRESTED SHIELD FERN

*a* A pinna                    *b* Portion of fertile pinna

169

Boott's Shield Fern is found in moist woods and near ponds. It is distinguished by its long, narrow fronds and minutely glandular indusium.

## 42. CRESTED SHIELD FERN

*Aspidium cristatum* (*Dryopteris cristata*)

Newfoundland to Kentucky, in swamps.  One to more than three feet high, with stalks which are chaffy, especially below, and which have light-brown scales, stalks of sterile fronds much shorter than those of fertile fronds.

*Fronds.*—Linear-oblong or lance-shaped, nearly twice-pinnate, fertile ones taller and longer stalked than the sterile ; *pinnæ* (of the fertile frond, turning their faces toward the apex of the frond) rather short, lance-shaped or triangular-oblong, deeply impressed with veins, cut deeply into oblong, obtuse, finely toothed divisions ; *fruit-dots* large, round, half-way between midvein and margin ; *indusium* large, flat.

In wet woods, growing either from the ground or from the trunks of fallen trees, and also in open meadows, we notice the tall, slender, dark-green, somewhat lustrous fronds of the Crested Shield Fern, usually distinguished easily from its kinsmen by the noticeably upward-turning pinnæ of the fertile fronds, and by the deep impression made by the veins on their upper surfaces.

The sterile fronds are much shorter than the fertile ones.  They are evergreen, lasting through the winter after the fertile fronds have perished.

Near the Crested Shield Fern we find often many of its kinsmen, broad, feathery fronds of the Spinulose Wood Fern, more slender ones of Boott's Shield

PLATE XXX

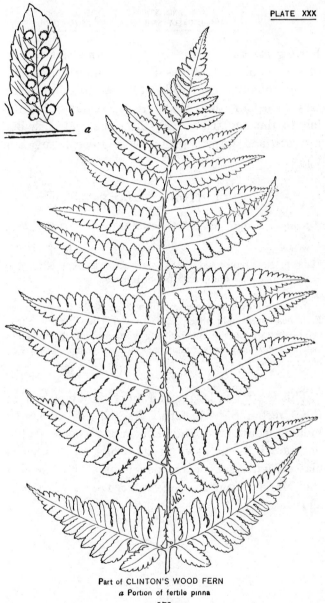

Part of CLINTON'S WOOD FERN
*a* Portion of fertile pinna

Fern, great tufts made by the magnificent bright-
green fronds of Goldie's Fern, symmetrical circles
of vigorous Evergreen Wood Fern, and shining clusters of the Christmas Fern. All these plants, belonging to the one tribe, seek the same moist, shaded
retreats, and form a group of singular beauty and
vigor.

### 43. CLINTON'S WOOD FERN

*Aspidium cristatum, var. Clintonianum (Dryopteris cristata Clinto-
niana)*

Maine to New Jersey and Pennsylvania, in swampy woods. Two
and a half to four feet high.

*Fronds.*—Larger in every way than those of the Crested Shield
Fern, nearly twice-pinnate; *pinnæ broadest at base*, cut into from
eight to sixteen pairs of linear-oblong, obtuse, obscurely toothed divisions; *fruit-dots* large, round, near the midvein; *indusium* orbicular, smooth.

This is a much larger and more showy plant than
the Crested Shield Fern. Its tall, broad, hardy-
looking fronds are found in our moist woods. While
not rare it is exclusive in its habits, and cannot be
classed with such every-day finds as its kinsmen,
the Marsh, Spinulose, Evergreen, and Christmas
Ferns.

PLATE XXXI

Part of fertile frond of Goldie's Fern
*a* Portion of a fertile pinna

## 44. GOLDIE'S FERN

*Aspidium Goldianum* (*Dryopteris Goldieana*)

New Brunswick to North Carolina and Tennessee, in rich woods. Two to more than four feet high, with stalks which are chaffy near the base.

*Fronds.*—Broadly ovate, the early sterile ones much broader in proportion and smaller, usually a foot or more wide, once-pinnate; *pinnæ* pinnatifid; *broadest in the middle* (the distinction from Clinton's Wood Fern), the divisions, about twenty pairs, oblong-linear, slightly toothed; *fruit-dots* very near the midvein; *indusium* very large, orbicular.

In the golden twilight of the deeper woods this stately plant unfurls its tall, broad, bright - green fronds, studded on their backs with the round fruit-dots which are so noticeable in this *Aspidium*, adding much to their attractiveness by the suggestion of fertility.

This plant ranks with the Osmundas and with the Ostrich Fern in size and vigorous beauty. Its retiring habits give it a reputation for rarity or at least for exclusiveness.

PLATE XXXII

EVERGREEN WOOD FERN

*a* Tip of fertile pinna          *b* Magnified fruit-dot, showing indusium and sporangia

175

## 45. EVERGREEN WOOD FERN. MARGINAL SHIELD FERN

*Aspidium marginale* (*Dryopteris marginalis*)

Canada to Alabama, in rocky woods.   A few inches to three feet
high, with more or less chaffy stalks having shining scales.

*Fronds.*—Ovate-oblong, smooth, thick, somewhat leathery, once
or twice-pinnate ; *pinnæ* lance-shaped or triangular-ovate, tapering
at the end, cut into pinnules ; *pinnules* oblong, entire, or toothed ;
*fruit-dots* large, round, close to the margin; *indusium* large, convex, persistent.

Above the black leaf-mould in our rocky northern
woods rise the firm, graceful crowns formed by the
blue-green fronds of the Evergreen Wood Fern.
The plant bears a family likeness to the Crested
Shield Fern, but its conspicuously marginal fruit-
dots identify it at sight.

It is interesting to read that it comes "nearer
being a tree-fern than any other of our species, the
caudex covered by the bases of fronds of previous
seasons, sometimes resting on bare rocks for four
or five inches without roots or fronds" (see Eaton,
p. 70).   This peculiarity in the plant's growth is
often striking and certainly suggests the tree-ferns
of the green-house.

Frequently in this species I notice what is more
or less common to nearly all ferns, the exquisite
contrast in the different shades of green worn by
the younger and older fronds and the charming
effect produced when the deep green of the centre
of a frond shades away in the most delicate manner
toward its apex and the tips of its pinnules.

As its English title signifies, the Evergreen Wood

Fern flourishes throughout the winter. In one of
the October entries in his journal, Thoreau records
his satisfaction in the endurance of the hardy ferns:
" Now they are conspicuous amid the withered
leaves. You are inclined to approach and raise each
frond in succession, moist, trembling, fragile greenness. They linger thus in all moist, clammy swamps
under the bare maples and grapevines and witch
hazels, and about each trickling spring that is half
choked with fallen leaves. What means this persistent vitality? Why were these spared when the
brakes and osmundas were stricken down? They
stay as if to keep up the spirits of the cold-blooded
frogs which have not yet gone into the mud, that
the summer may die with decent and graceful mod-
eration. Is not the water of the spring improved
by their presence? They fall back and droop here
and there like the plumes of departing summer, of
the departing year. Even in them I feel an argu-
ment for immortality. Death is so far from being
universal. The same destroyer does not destroy
all. How valuable they are, with the lycopodiums,
for cheerfulness. Greenness at the end of the year,
after the fall of the leaf, a hale old age. To my eye
they are tall and noble as palm-groves, and always
some forest nobleness seems to have its haunt under
their umbrage. All that was immortal in the swamp
herbage seems here crowded into smaller compass,
the concentrated greenness of the swamp. How dear
they must be to the chickadee and the rabbit! the cool,
slowly retreating rear-guard of the swamp army."

## 46. FRAGRANT SHIELD FERN

*Aspidium fragrans* (*Dryopteris fragrans*)

Northern New England to Wisconsin and northward, on rocks.
Five to sixteen inches long, with very chaffy stalks having
brown, glossy scales.

*Fronds.*—Lance-shaped, tapering to a point, nearly twice-pinnate,
fragrant; *pinnæ* oblong-lanceolate, pinnatifid; *fruit-dots* round,
large; *indusium* large and thin.

The Fragrant Shield Fern thrives in a colder
climate than that chosen by many of its kinsmen.
Though found in the White Mountains, in the
Green Mountains (where it climbs to an elevation
of four thousand feet), in the Adirondacks, and in
other special localities of about the same latitude,
yet it is rare till we journey farther north. It loves
the crevices of shaded cliffs or mossy rocks, often
thriving best in the neighborhood of rushing brooks
and waterfalls. Frequently it seems to seek the most
inaccessible spots, as if anxious to evade discovery.
Mr. J. A. Bates, of Randolph, Vt., writes that he first
saw this little plant through a telescope from the
piazza of the Summit House on Mount Mansfield on
an apparently inaccessible ledge, the only instance in
my experience when the fern student has sought this
method of observation, suggesting " Ferns Through
a Spy-glass" as a companion volume to "Birds
Through an Opera-glass." But even the most carefully chosen spots are not safe from invasion, as Mr.
Bates tells us, for some unprincipled persons, having
felled neighboring trees and constructed a rude lad-

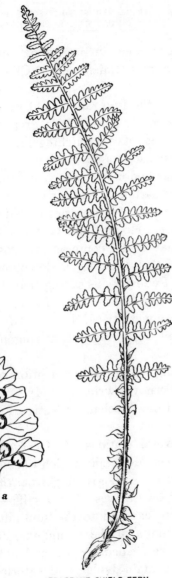

FRAGRANT SHIELD FERN
*a* Portion of fertile pinna

179

der, have succeeded in uprooting every plant
from the Fragrant Shield Fern Cliff on Mount
Mansfield.

The fronds of the Fragrant Shield Fern grow in a
crown and the fertile ones fruit in great abundance.

Eaton writes as follows touching the fragrance of
this fern and its use as a beverage:

"The pleasant odor of this plant remains many
years in the herbarium. The early writers compare
the fragrance to that of raspberries, and Milde repeats
the observation. Hooker and Greville thought it
'not unlike that of the common primrose.' Maxi-
mowicz states that the odor is sometimes lacking.
Milde quotes Redowsky as saying that the Yakoots
of Siberia use the plant in place of tea; and, having
tried the experiment myself, I can testify to the not
unpleasant and very fragrant astringency of the
infusion."

The following delightful description of the Fragrant Shield Fern was written by Mr. C. G. Pringle,
and is taken from Meehan's "Native Flowers and
Ferns":

"In the several stations of *Aspidium fragrans*
among the Green Mountains which I have explored,
the plant is always seen growing from the crevices
or on the narrow shelves of dry cliffs—not often
such cliffs as are exposed to the sunlight, unless it
be on the summits of the mountains, but usually
such cliffs as are shaded by firs, and notably such
as overhang mountain-rivulets and waterfalls. When
I visit such places in summer, the niches occupied

by the plants are quite dry. I think it would be
fatal to the plant if much spray should fall on it
during the season of its active growth. When you
enter the shade and solitude of the haunts of this
fern, its presence is betrayed by its resinous odor;
looking up the face of the cliff, usually mottled with
lichens and moss, you see it often far above your
reach hanging against the rock, masses of dead
brown fronds, the accumulations of many years, preserved by the resinous principle which pervades
them; for the fronds, as they disport regularly
about the elongating caudex, fall right and left pre-
cisely like a woman's hair. Above the tuft of droop-
ing dead fronds, which radiate from the centre of
the plant, grow from six to twenty green fronds,
which represent the growth of the season, those of
the preceding year dying toward autumn."

## 47. BRAUN'S HOLLY FERN

*Aspidium aculeatum*, var. *Braunii* (*Dryopteris Braunii*)

Canada to Maine, the mountains of Pennsylvania and westward, in deep rocky woods. One to more than two feet long, with chaffy stalks, having brown scales.

*Fronds.*—Thick, twice-pinnate; *pinnæ* lanceolate, tapering both ways; *pinnules* covered with hairs and scales, truncate, nearly rectangular at the base; *fruit-dots* roundish, small, mostly near the midveins; *indusium* orbicular, entire.

This fern is said to have been first discovered by Frederick Pursh in 1807 in Smuggler's Notch, Mount Mansfield, Vt. In the Green Mountains and in the Catskills several stations have been established. It has been found also in the Adirondacks and in Oswego County, N. Y., and it is now reported as common in the rocky woods of northern Maine, and by mountain brooks in northern New England.

Braun's Holly Fern is one of the numerous varieties of the Prickly Shield Fern or *A. aculeatum* (*D. aculeata*).

Though few of our fern-students will have an opportunity to follow the Prickly Shield Fern through all the forms it assumes in different parts of the world, yet undoubtedly many of them will have the pleasure of seeing in one of its lonely and lovely haunts our own variety, Braun's Holly Fern.

PLATE XXXIV

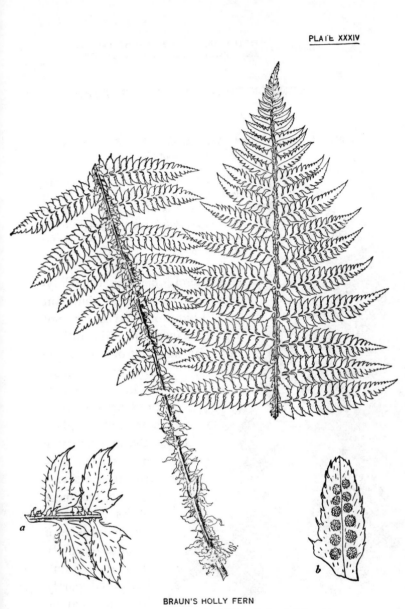

**BRAUN'S HOLLY FERN**

*a* Portion of pinna        *b* Fertile pinnule, indusia gone

## 48. COMMON POLYPODY. SNAKE FERN

*Polypodium vulgare*

Almost throughout North America, on rocks.    A few inches to
more than a foot high.

*Fronds.*—Oblong, smooth, somewhat leathery, cut into narrowly oblong, usually obtuse divisions which almost reach the rachis ; *fruit-dots* large, round, half-way between the midrib and margin; *indusium*, none.

Strangely enough, the Polypody, one of our most abundant and ubiquitous ferns, is not rightly named, if it is noticed at all, by nine out of ten people who come across it in the woods or along the roadside. Yet the plant has a charm peculiarly its own, a charm arising partly from its vigor, from the freshness of its youth and the endurance of its old age, partly from its odd outlines, and partly from its usual environment, which

Polypody

184

entitles it to a more ready and universal recognition.

"The cheerful community of the polypody," as Thoreau calls it, thrives best on the flat surfaces of rocks. I recall the base of certain great cliffs where the rocky fragments, looking as though hurled from above by playful giants, are thickly covered with these plants, their rich foliage softening into beauty otherwise rugged outlines. Usually the plant is found in somewhat shaded places. Occasionally it grows on the trunks of trees and on fallen logs, as well as on rocks and cliffs.

A few weeks ago I found its fronds prettily curtaining the cleverly hidden nest of a pair of black and white creepers. It is with good reason that these birds are noted for their skill in concealing their dwelling-place. This special afternoon, when persuaded by their

*a*

Tip of fertile frond

nervous chirps and flutterings about the rocky perch where I was sitting that the young ones were close by, I began an investigation of my precipitous and very slippery surroundings which was not rewarded for an hour or more. Not till I had climbed several feet over the side of the cliff to a narrow shelf below, broken through a thicket of blueberries, and pushed aside the tufts of Polypody which hid the entrance to the dark crevice in the rocks beyond, did I discover the little nest holding the baby creepers.

Thoreau writes of the Polypody with peculiar
sympathy:

" It is very pleasant and cheerful nowadays, when
the brown and withered leaves strew the ground
and almost every plant is fallen withered, to come
upon a patch of polypody . . . on some rocky
hill-side in the woods, where, in the midst of dry
and rustling leaves, defying frost, it stands so
freshly green and full of life.  The mere greenness,
which was not remarkable in the summer, is posi-
tively interesting now.  My thoughts are with the
polypody a long time after my body has passed.
. . . Why is not this form copied by our sculp-
tors instead of the foreign acanthus leaves and
bays?  How fit for a tuft about the base of a col-
umn!  The sight of this unwithering green leaf ex-
cites me like red at some seasons.  Are not wood-
frogs the philosophers who frequent these groves?
Methinks I imbibe a cool, composed, frog-like philosophy when I behold them.  The form of the polypody is strangely interesting, it is even outlandish.
Some forms, though common in our midst, are thus
perennially foreign as the growth of other latitudes.
. . . The bare outline of the polypody thrills me
strangely.  It only perplexes me.  Simple as it is, it
is as strange as an oriental character.  It is quite
independent of my race and of the Indian, and of
all mankind.  It is a fabulous, mythological form,
such as prevailed when the earth and air and
water were inhabited by those extinct fossil creat-
ures that we find.  It is contemporary with them,

and affects us somewhat as the sight of them
might do."

### 49. LONG BEECH FERN

*Phegopteris polypodioides* (*P. Phegopteris*)

Newfoundland to Alaska, south to mountains of
Virginia, wet woods and hill-sides.    Six or eight inches
to more than a foot high.

*Fronds.*—Triangular, usually longer than broad
(4–9 inches long, 3–6 inches broad), downy, especially
beneath, thin, once-pinnate ; *pinnæ* lance-shaped, the
lower pair noticeably standing forward and deflexed,
cut into oblong, obtuse seg-
ments ; *fruit-dots* small, round,
near the margin ; *indusium*,
none.

Of the three species
of *Phegopteris* native to
the northeastern States
*P. polypodioides*, com-
monly called the Long
Beech Fern, is the one
I happen to have en-
countered oftenest.

It is a less delicate
plant than either of its
sisters, the effect of the
larger and older specimens being
rather hardy, yet its downy, often
light-green, triangular frond is ex-
ceedingly pretty, with a certain oddity of aspect which it owes to the

Long Beech Fern

187

lowest pair of pinnæ, these being conspicuously
deflexed and turned forward. This peculiarity
gives it a decided individuality and renders it easy
of identification.

The Long Beech Fern I have found growing

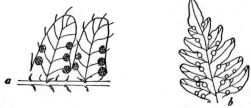

*a* Portion of pinna                *b* Tip of pinna

alternately in company with the Oak Fern and the
Broad Beech Fern. It loves the damp woods,
clambering over the roots of trees or carpeting
thickly the hollows that lie between.

### 50. BROAD BEECH FERN. HEXAGON BEECH FERN

*Phegopteris hexagonoptera*

Quebec to Florida, in dry woods and on hill-sides, with stalks
eight to eighteen inches long.

*Fronds.*—Triangular, as broad or broader than long, seven to
twelve inches broad, thin, slightly hairy, often finely glandular beneath, fragrant, once-pinnate; *pinnæ*, the large, lowest ones broadest near the middle and cut nearly to the midrib into linear-
oblong, obtuse segments, the middle ones lance-shaped, tapering,
the upper ones oblong, obtuse, toothed or entire; *basal segments*
of the pinnæ forming a continuous, many-angled wing along the
main rachis; *fruit-dots* round, small, near the margin; *indusium*,
none.

In many ways this plant resembles its sister, the
Long Beech Fern, but usually it is a larger plant,

PLATE XXXV

BROAD BEECH FERN

with more broadly triangular fronds, which wear, to
my mind, a brighter, fresher, more delicate green.
In the Long Beech Fern the two lower pairs of pinnæ differ little in length and breadth, while in the
Broad Beech Fern the lowest pair are decidedly
larger and broader than the next pair. The wing
along the rachis formed by the basal segments of the
pinnæ seems to me more conspicuous in the latter
than in the former.

The range of the Broad Beech Fern extends farther south than does that of its two kinsmen, neither
of which are found, I believe, south of Virginia. It
seeks also more open and usually drier woods. Its
leaves are fragrant.

Williamson says that its fronds are easily decolor-
ized and that they form a "good object for double-
staining, a process well known to microscopists."

### 51. OAK FERN

*Phegopteris Dryopteris*

Northeastern United States to Virginia, west to Oregon and
Alaska, usually in wet woods, with stalks six to nine inches long.

*Fronds.*—Usually longer than broad, four to nine inches long,
broadly triangular, the three primary divisions widely spreading,
smooth, once or twice-pinnate ; *fruit-dots* small, round, near the
margin ; *indusium*, none.

So far as I remember, my first encounter with the
Oak Fern was in a cedar swamp, famous for its
growth of showy lady's-slippers. One July day
in the hope of finding in flower some of these

PLATE XXXVI

OAK FERN

191

orchids, I visited this swamp. It lay in a semi-
twilight, caused by the dense growth of cedars and
hemlocks. Prostrate on the spongy sphagnum below were hosts of uprooted trees, so overrun with
trailing strands of partridge-vine, twin-flower, gold-
thread, and creeping snowberry, and so soft and
yielding to the feet that they seemed to have become one with the earth. The stumps and far-
reaching roots of the trees that had been cut or
broken off above ground, instead of having been
uprooted bodily, had also become gardens of many
delicate woodland growths. Some of these decaying stumps and outspreading roots were thickly
clothed with the clover-like leaflets of the wood-
sorrel, here and there nestling among them a pink-
veined blossom. On others I found side by side
gleaming wild strawberries and dwarf raspberries,
feathery fronds of Maidenhair, tall Osmundas, the
Crested and the Spinulose Shield Ferns, the leaves
of the violet, foam-flower, mitrewort, and many
others of the smaller, wood-loving plants. Among
these stumps were pools of water filled with the
dark, polished, rounded leaves of the wild calla,
and bordered by beds of moss which cushioned the
equally shining but long and pointed leaves of the
*Clintonia*. Near one of these pools grew a patch
of delicate, low-spreading plants, evidently ferns.
It needed only one searching look at the broad,
triangular, light-green fronds—suggesting somewhat
those of a small Brake—with roundish fruit-dots below to assure me that I had found the Oak Fern.

Every lover of plants or of birds or of any natural objects will appreciate the sense of something more exciting than satisfaction which I experienced as I knelt above the little plantation and gathered a few slender-stemmed fronds. One such find as this compensates for many hours of fatigue and discomfort, or intensifies the enjoyment of an already happy day. The expedition had justified itself with the first full view of the solemn, beautiful depths of the cedar forest. The discovery of the Oak Fern provided a tangible token of what we had accomplished, and when finally we found the tall, leafy plants of the showy lady's-slipper, without a single blossom left upon them, our disappointment was so mild as to be almost imperceptible.

As is often the case, having once discovered the haunt of the Oak Fern, it ceased to be a rarity. It joined the host of plants which climbed over the mossy stumps and fallen logs, and at times it fairly carpeted the ground beneath the cedars and hemlocks.

## 52. BULBLET BLADDER FERN

*Cystopteris bulbifera*

Canada to Tennessee, on wet rocks, preferring limestone. One to three feet long, with light-colored, somewhat brittle stalks.

*Fronds.*—Elongated, lance-shaped from a broad base, often bearing beneath large, fleshy bulbs, usually twice-pinnate; *pinnæ* lance-oblong, pointed; *pinnules* toothed or deeply lobed; *fruit-dots* roundish, *indusium* short, hood-like, attached by a broad base on the side toward the midrib, early thrown back and withering so that the mature fruit-dots appear arched.

The Bulblet Bladder Fern is never more at home than when it grows close to falling water, clinging to rocks dark and wet with spray. It seems to reflect

PLATE XXXVII

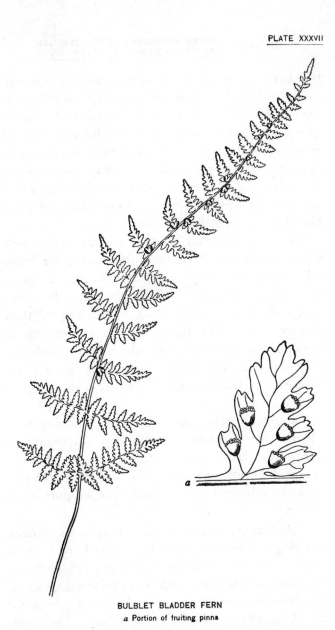

**BULBLET BLADDER FERN**
*a* Portion of fruiting pinna

195

the very spirit of the waterfall, all its life and
grace, as it springs from the dripping ledges, clothing them with a diaphanous garment of delicate
green which vies with their neighboring veil of
white, now pouring over some rocky shelf a solid
but silent mass of pale luxuriant foliage, now trailing
down the cliff its long, tapering fronds, side by side
with silvery strands of water, close to tufts of wind-
blown, spray-tipped hare-bells.

Although the plant is never seen at its best save
in some such neigh'borhood as this, its slender, feathery fronds are always possessed of singular grace
and charm, whether undulating along the dried
rocky bed of a mountain brook or bending till their
slender tips nearly touch the rushing stream or
growing quite away from the rocks which are
their natural and usual companions among the
moss-grown trunks and fallen trees of the wet
woods.

I know no other fern, save the climbing fern,
which is so vine-like and clinging. In reality its
stalk and midrib are somewhat brittle, yet this brit-
tleness does not prevent its adapting itself with sup-
ple and exquisite curves to whatever support it has
chosen.

In its manner of growth, as well as in its slender,
tapering outline, the Bulblet Bladder Fern is so in-
dividual that there can be no difficulty in identifying
the full-sized fertile fronds, even in the absence of
the little bulbs which grow on the under side of the
frond, usually at the base of the pinnæ. The sterile

PLATE XXXVIII

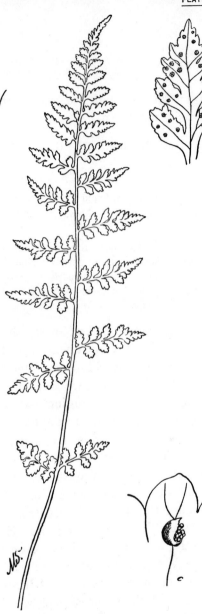

**FRAGILE BLADDER FERN**

*a* Portion of fertile pinna        *b* Tip of fertile pinna
*c* Magnified fruit-dot showing indusium

197

fronds are shorter and broader in proportion, and
not so easily identified.

### 53. FRAGILE BLADDER FERN. COMMON BLADDER FERN

*Cystopteris fragilis*

A rock and wood fern, found from Newfoundland to Georgia.
Six to eighteen inches long, with slender and brittle stalks, green
except at the base.

*Fronds.*—Oblong-lanceolate, thin, twice to thrice-pinnate or pinnatifid ; *pinnæ* lance-ovate, irregularly cut into toothed segments
which at their base run along the midrib by a narrow margin ; *fruit-
dots* roundish, often abundant; *indusium* early withering and
exposing the sporangia, which finally appear naked.

This plant may be ranked among the earliest ferns
of the year. In May or June, if we climb down to
the brook where the columbine flings out her brilliant, nodding blossoms, we find the delicate little
fronds, just uncurled, clinging to the steep, moist
rocks, or perhaps beyond, in the deeper woods, they
nestle among the spreading roots of some great forest tree. Their "fragile greenness" is very winning.
As the plant matures, attaining at times a height of
nearly two feet, it loses something of this first delicate charm. By the end of July its fruit has ripened,
its spores are discharged, and the plant disappears.
Frequently, if not always, a new crop springs up in
August. We are enchanted to discover tender
young fronds making patches of fresh green in every crevice of the rocks among which the stream
forces its precipitous way. Once more the woods
are flavored with the essence of spring. In our

PLATE XXXIX

RUSTY WOODSIA

delight in this new promise we forget for a moment to mourn the vanishing summer.

The outline of the Common Bladder Fern suggests that of the Obtuse Woodsia. The two plants
might be difficult to distinguish were it not for the
difference in their indusia. At maturity the indusium of the Common Bladder Fern usually disappears, leaving the fruit-dot naked, while that of the
Obtuse Woodsia is fastened underneath the fruit-
dot and splits apart into jagged, spreading lobes.

The sterile fronds of the Slender Cliff Brake also
have been thought to resemble this fern, in whose
company it often grows.

Williamson says that the Common Bladder Fern
is easily cultivated either in mounds or on rock-
work.

### 54. RUSTY WOODSIA

*Woodsia Ilvensis*

From Labrador and Greenland south to North Carolina and Kentucky, usually on exposed rocks in somewhat mountainous regions.
A few inches to nearly one foot high.

*Fronds.*—Oblong-lance-shaped, rather smooth above, the stalk
and under surface of the frond thickly clothed with rusty chaff,
once-pinnate ; *pinnæ* oblong, obtuse, sessile, cut into oblong segments ; *fruit-dots* round, near the margin, often confluent at maturity ; *indusium* detached by its base under the sporangia, dividing
into slender hairs which curl above them.

Last Decoration Day, while clambering over
some rocky cliffs in the Berkshire Hills, I found the
Rusty Woodsia growing in masses so luxuriant to
the eye and so velvety to the touch that it hardly

PLATE XL

**BLUNT-LOBED WOODSIA**

*a* Portion of pinna          *b* Fruit-dot magnified, showing indusium

suggested the bristly looking plant which one finds
later in the summer.

This fern reverses the usual order of things, being gray-haired in youth and brown-haired in old
age, with the result that in May its effect is a soft,
silvery green.   But even in August, if you chance
upon a vigorous tuft springing from some rocky
crevice, despite its lack of delicacy and its bristle
of red-brown hairs or chaff, the plant is an attractive one.

Environment has much to do with the charm of
ferns.   The first plant of this species I ever identified grew on a rocky shelf within a few feet of a
stream which flowed swift and cold from the near
mountains.   Close by, from the forked branches of
a crimson-fruited mountain maple, hung the dainty,
deserted nest of a vireo.   Always the Rusty Woodsia seems to bring me a message from that abode
of solitude and silence.

### 55. BLUNT-LOBED WOODSIA

*Woodsia obtusa*

Canada to Georgia and Alabama and westward, on rocks.
Eight to twenty inches high, with stalks not jointed, chaffy when
young.

*Fronds.*—Broadly lanceolate, nearly twice-pinnate ; *pinnæ* rather
remote, triangular-ovate or oblong, pinnately parted into obtuse,
oblong, toothed segments ; *veins* forked ; *fruit-dots* on or near
the minutely toothed lobes ; *indusium* conspicuous, splitting into
several jagged lobes.

The Blunt-lobed Woodsia is not rare on rocks and
stony hillsides in Maine and Northern New York.

It is found frequently in the valley of the Hudson.
Though not related to the Common Bladder Fern
(*C. fragilis*), it has somewhat the same general appearance. Its fronds, however, are usually both
broader and longer, and its stalk and pinnæ are
slightly downy. Its range does not vary greatly
from that of the Common Bladder Fern, but
usually it grows in more exposed spots and sometimes basks in strong sunshine.

Meehan says the Blunt-lobed Woodsia is found
along the Wissahickon Creek, Penna., on dry walls
in shady places. " One of its happiest phases,"
he continues, " is toward the fall of the year, when
the short, barren fronds which form the outer circle
bend downward, forming a sort of rosette, in the
centre of which the fertile fronds somewhat erectly
stand."

The sterile fronds remain fairly green till spring.

### 56. NORTHERN WOODSIA. ALPINE WOODSIA

*Woodsia hyperborea* ( *W. alpina* )

Northern New York and Vermont, and northward from Labrador to Alaska, on rocks. Two to six inches long, with stalks
jointed near the base.

*Fronds.*—Narrowly oblong-lanceolate, nearly smooth, pinnate ;
*pinnæ* triangular-ovate, obtuse, lobed ; *lobes* few ; *fruit-dots* somewhat scattered ; *indusium* as in *W. Ilvensis.*

This rare little fern has been found by Dr. Peck
in the Adirondacks and by Horace Mann, jr., and
Mr. Pringle in Vermont. In his delightful " Rem-

iniscences of Botanical Rambles in Vermont,"
published in the Torrey *Bulletin*, July, 1897, Mr.
Pringle describes his first discovery of this species:

" I was on the mountain [Willoughby] on the 4th
of August and examined the entire length of the
cliffs, climbing upon all their accessible shelves.
Among the specimens of *Woodsia glabella* brought
away were a few which I judged to belong to a
different species. Mr. Frost, to whom they were
first submitted, pronounced them *Woodsia glabella*.
Not satisfied with his report, I showed them to Dr.
Gray. By him I was advised to send them to Professor Eaton, because, as he said, *Woodsia* is a critical genus. Professor Eaton assured me that I had
*Woodsia hyperborea*, . . . another addition to the
flora of the United States."

Later in the year Mr. Pringle made a visit to
Smugglers' Notch on Mount Mansfield, when he was
"prepared to camp in the old Notch House among
hedgehogs, and botanize the region day by day."
This visit was rich in its results. The most nota-
ble finds were *Aspidium fragrans, Asplenium viride,
Woodsia glabella*, and *Woodsia hyperborea*.

PLATE XLi

NORTHERN WOODSIA

## 57. SMOOTH WOODSIA

*Woodsia glabella*

Northern New York and Vermont, and northward from Labrador to Alaska, on moist rocks. Two to five inches long, with stalks jointed at base.

*Fronds.*—Very delicate, linear or narrowly lanceolate, smooth on both sides, pinnate; *pinnæ* roundish ovate, obtuse, lobed, lobes few; *fruit-dots* scattered; *indusium* minute.

The Smooth Woodsia closely resembles the Northern Woodsia, and one may expect to find it in much the same parts of the country. In texture it is still more delicate; its fronds are almost perfectly smooth, its outline is narrower, and its pinnæ are but slightly lobed.

Mr. Pringle tells us that a letter from Mr. George Davenport, asking him to look for *Woodsia glabella*, awakened his first interest in ferns. His own account of these early fern hunts is inspiring in its enthusiasm:

"In 1873 George Davenport was beginning his study of ferns. A letter from him, asking me to look for *Woodsia glabella* . . . started me on a fern hunt. The species had been found on Willoughby Mountain, Vt., and at Little Falls, N. Y.; might it not be growing in many places in Vermont? When I set out I knew, as I must suppose, not a single fern, and it was near the close of the summer. You can imagine what delights awaited me in the autumn woodlands. I made the acquaintance of not a few ferns, though it was too late to prepare good specimens of them. In this first blind endeavor I got, of

PLATE XLII

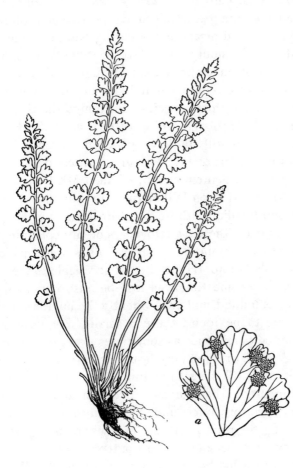

SMOOTH WOODSIA
*a* Fertile pinna
207

course, no clew to *Woodsia glabella*. The next summer the hunt was renewed and persistently followed up. I found pleasure in securing one by one nearly all our Vermont ferns. At the time I thought it worthy of remembrance that a single field of diversified pasture and woodland on an adjoining farm yielded me thirty species. Although the two common species of *Woodsia* were near at hand, *Woodsia glabella* was still eluding my search. I sent a friend to the summit of Jay Peak in a fruitless quest for it. Finally, on September 1st, I joined Mr. Congdon at its old station on Willoughby Mountain, and made myself familiar with its exquisite form.

"During the first two years of my collecting in earnest, 1874 and 1875, several visits were made to Camel's Hump, the peak most accessible to me. In this way some time was lost, because its subalpine area is limited, and consequently the number of rare plants to be found there is small. Yet, with such dogged persistence as sometimes prevents my making good progress, my last visit to that point was not made till the 20th of June, 1876. On that day I clambered, I believe, over every shelf of its great southern precipice and peered into every fissure among the rocks. At last, as I was climbing up the apex over the southeastern buttress, my perilous toil was rewarded by the discovery not only of *Woodsia glabella*, but of *Aspidium fragrans*. . . . There were only a few depauperate specimens of each which had not yet succumbed to the adverse conditions of their dry and exposed situation."

In the following passage Mr. Pringle describes his
pleasure, some years later, in the companionships
fostered by a common interest in his pet hobby:

". . . my delight in this preserve of boreal
plants was shared with not a few genial botanists.
Charles Faxon came before any of us suspected that
he possessed undeveloped talent for a botanical artist of highest excellence. Edwin Faxon followed
his young brother, and with me made the tedious ascent to Stirling Pond, a day of toil well rewarded.
Thomas Morong came, before the hardships of his
Paraguayan journey had broken him down. . . .
Our honored President came. . . . In those days,
as now, . . . he was often my companion to add
delight to my occupation and to reinforce my enthusiasm. . . . The gentle Davenport came at
last to behold for the first time in their native haunts
many of the objects of his first love and study. When
I had found for him yet once more in a fifth Vermont
station (this was under Checkerberry Ledge, near
Bakersfield) the fern he at first desired, and, together
with that, had discovered within our limits three or
four others quite as rare and scarcely expected, I
might feel that I had complied with the request of his
letter. But that letter initiated a warm friendship
between us and association in work upon American
ferns, which has continued to the present time.
During these twenty-three years of botanical travel
on my part my hands have gathered all but thirty-
six of the one hundred and sixty-five species of North
American ferns, and from the more remote corners

of our continent I have sent home to my friend for
description and publication sixteen new ones.  Yet
I trust that the fern hunt upon which he started me
in 1873 is still far from its close."

The above quotations illustrate fairly the enthusiasm aroused by a pursuit which is full of peculiar
fascination.  Almost anyone who has made a study
of our native ferns will recall hours filled with delight through their agency, companions made more
companionable by means of a common interest in
their names, haunts, and habits.

# INDEX TO LATIN NAMES

# INDEX TO LATIN NAMES

# INDEX TO ENGLISH NAMES

213

# INDEX TO TECHNICAL TERMS

# A CATALOGUE OF SELECTED DOVER BOOKS
# IN ALL FIELDS OF INTEREST

# A CATALOGUE OF SELECTED DOVER BOOKS
## IN ALL FIELDS OF INTEREST

LEATHER TOOLING AND CARVING, Chris H. Groneman. One of few books concentrating on tooling and carving, with complete instructions and grid designs for 39 projects ranging from bookmarks to bags. 148 illustrations. 111pp. 7⅞ x 10.
23061-9 Pa. $2.50

THE CODEX NUTTALL, A PICTURE MANUSCRIPT FROM ANCIENT MEXICO, as first edited by Zelia Nuttall. Only inexpensive edition, in full color, of a pre-Columbian Mexican (Mixtec) book. 88 color plates show kings, gods, heroes, temples, sacrifices. New explanatory, historical introduction by Arthur G. Miller. 96pp. 11⅜ x 8½.
23168-2 Pa. $7.50

AMERICAN PRIMITIVE PAINTING, Jean Lipman. Classic collection of an enduring American tradition. 109 plates, 8 in full color—portraits, landscapes, Biblical and historical scenes, etc., showing family groups, farm life, and so on. 80pp. of lucid text. 8⅜ x 11¼.
22815-0 Pa. $4.00

WILL BRADLEY: HIS GRAPHIC ART, edited by Clarence P. Hornung. Striking collection of work by foremost practitioner of Art Nouveau in America: posters, cover designs, sample pages, advertisements, other illustrations. 97 plates, including 8 in full color and 19 in two colors. 97pp. 9⅜ x 12¼.
20701-3 Pa. $4.00
22120-2 Clothbd. $10.00

THE UNDERGROUND SKETCHBOOK OF JAN FAUST, Jan Faust. 101 bitter, horrifying, black-humorous, penetrating sketches on sex, war, greed, various liberations, etc. Sometimes sexual, but not pornographic. Not for prudish. 101pp. 6½ x 9¼.
22740-5 Pa. $1.50

THE GIBSON GIRL AND HER AMERICA, Charles Dana Gibson. 155 finest drawings of effervescent world of 1900-1910: the Gibson Girl and her loves, amusements, adventures, Mr. Pipp, etc. Selected by E. Gillon; introduction by Henry Pitz. 144pp. 8¼ x 11⅜.
21986-0 Pa. $3.50

STAINED GLASS CRAFT, J.A.F. Divine, G. Blachford. One of the very few books that tell the beginner exactly what he needs to know: planning cuts, making shapes, avoiding design weaknesses, fitting glass, etc. 93 illustrations. 115pp.
22812-6 Pa. $1.50

AUSTRIAN COOKING AND BAKING, Gretel Beer. Authentic thick soups, wiener schnitzel, veal goulash, more, plus dumplings, puff pastries, nut cakes, sacher tortes, other great Austrian desserts. 224pp. USO 23220-4 Pa. $2.50

CHEESES OF THE WORLD, U.S.D.A. Dictionary of cheeses containing descriptions of over 400 varieties of cheese from common Cheddar to exotic Surati. Up to two pages are given to important cheeses like Camembert, Cottage, Edam, etc. 151pp. 22831-2 Pa. $1.50

TRITTON'S GUIDE TO BETTER WINE AND BEER MAKING FOR BEGINNERS, S.M. Tritton. All you need to know to make family-sized quantities of over 100 types of grape, fruit, herb, vegetable wines; plus beers, mead, cider, more. 11 illustrations. 157pp. USO 22528-3 Pa. $2.00

DECORATIVE LABELS FOR HOME CANNING, PRESERVING, AND OTHER HOUSEHOLD AND GIFT USES, Theodore Menten. 128 gummed, perforated labels, beautifully printed in 2 colors. 12 versions in traditional, Art Nouveau, Art Deco styles. Adhere to metal, glass, wood, most plastics. 24pp. 8¼ x 11. 23219-0 Pa. $2.00

FIVE ACRES AND INDEPENDENCE, Maurice G. Kains. Great back-to-the-land classic explains basics of self-sufficient farming: economics, plants, crops, animals, orchards, soils, land selection, host of other necessary things. Do not confuse with skimpy faddist literature; Kains was one of America's greatest agriculturalists. 95 illustrations. 397pp. 20974-1 Pa. $2.95

GROWING VEGETABLES IN THE HOME GARDEN, U.S. Dept. of Agriculture. Basic information on site, soil conditions, selection of vegetables, planting, cultivation, gathering. Up-to-date, concise, authoritative. Covers 60 vegetables. 30 illustrations. 123pp. 23167-4 Pa. $1.35

FRUITS FOR THE HOME GARDEN, Dr. U.P. Hedrick. A chapter covering each type of garden fruit, advice on plant care, soils, grafting, pruning, sprays, transplanting, and much more! Very full. 53 illustrations. 175pp. 22944-0 Pa. $2.50

GARDENING ON SANDY SOIL IN NORTH TEMPERATE AREAS, Christine Kelway. Is your soil too light, too sandy? Improve your soil, select plants that survive under such conditions. Both vegetables and flowers. 42 photos. 148pp. USO 23199-2 Pa. $2.50

THE FRAGRANT GARDEN: A BOOK ABOUT SWEET SCENTED FLOWERS AND LEAVES, Louise Beebe Wilder. Fullest, best book on growing plants for their fragrances. Descriptions of hundreds of plants, both well-known and overlooked. 407pp. 23071-6 Pa. $3.50

EASY GARDENING WITH DROUGHT-RESISTANT PLANTS, Arno and Irene Nehrling. Authoritative guide to gardening with plants that require a minimum of water: seashore, desert, and rock gardens; house plants; annuals and perennials; much more. 190 illustrations. 320pp. 23230-1 Pa. $3.50

CONSTRUCTION OF AMERICAN FURNITURE TREASURES, Lester Margon. 344 detail drawings, complete text on constructing exact reproductions of 38 early American masterpieces: Hepplewhite sideboard, Duncan Phyfe drop-leaf table, mantel clock, gate-leg dining table, Pa. German cupboard, more. 38 plates. 54 photographs. 168pp. 8⅜ x 11¼.
23056-2 Pa. $4.00

JEWELRY MAKING AND DESIGN, Augustus F. Rose, Antonio Cirino. Professional secrets revealed in thorough, practical guide: tools, materials, processes; rings, brooches, chains, cast pieces, enamelling, setting stones, etc. Do not confuse with skimpy introductions: beginner can use, professional can learn from it. Over 200 illustrations. 306pp.
21750-7 Pa. $3.00

METALWORK AND ENAMELLING, Herbert Maryon. Generally coneeded best all-around book. Countless trade secrets: materials, tools, soldering, filigree, setting, inlay, niello, repoussé, casting, polishing, etc. For beginner or expert. Author was foremost British expert. 330 illustrations. 335pp.
22702-2 Pa. $3.50

WEAVING WITH FOOT-POWER LOOMS, Edward F. Worst. Setting up a loom, beginning to weave, constructing equipment, using dyes, more, plus over 285 drafts of traditional patterns including Colonial and Swedish weaves. More than 200 other figures. For beginning and advanced. 275pp. 8¾ x 6⅜.
23064-3 Pa. $4.00

WEAVING A NAVAJO BLANKET, Gladys A. Reichard. Foremost anthropologist studied under Navajo women, reveals every step in process from wool, dyeing, spinning, setting up loom, designing, weaving. Much history, symbolism. With this book you could make one yourself. 97 illustrations. 222pp. 22992-0 Pa. $3.00

NATURAL DYES AND HOME DYEING, Rita J. Adrosko. Use natural ingredients: bark, flowers, leaves, lichens, insects etc. Over 135 specific recipes from historical sources for cotton, wool, other fabrics. Genuine premodern handicrafts. 12 illustrations. 160pp.
22688-3 Pa. $2.00

THE HAND DECORATION OF FABRICS, Francis J. Kafka. Outstanding, profusely illustrated guide to stenciling, batik, block printing, tie dyeing, freehand painting, silk screen printing, and novelty decoration. 356 illustrations. 198pp. 6 x 9.
21401-X Pa. $3.00

THOMAS NAST: CARTOONS AND ILLUSTRATIONS, with text by Thomas Nast St. Hill. Father of American political cartooning. Cartoons that destroyed Tweed Ring; inflation, free love, church and state; original Republican elephant and Democratic donkey; Santa Claus; more. 117 illustrations. 146pp. 9 x 12.
22983-1 Pa. $4.00
23067-8 Clothbd. $8.50

FREDERIC REMINGTON: 173 DRAWINGS AND ILLUSTRATIONS. Most famous of the Western artists, most responsible for our myths about the American West in its untamed days. Complete reprinting of Drawings of Frederic Remington (1897), plus other selections. 4 additional drawings in color on covers. 140pp. 9 x 12.
20714-5 Pa. $3.95

DECORATIVE ALPHABETS AND INITIALS, edited by Alexander Nesbitt. 91 complete alphabets (medieval to modern), 3924 decorative initials, including Victorian novelty and Art Nouveau. 192pp. 7¾ x 10¾. 20544-4 Pa. $3.50

CALLIGRAPHY, Arthur Baker. Over 100 original alphabets from the hand of our greatest living calligrapher: simple, bold, fine-line, richly ornamented, etc. —all strikingly original and different, a fusion of many influences and styles. 155pp. 11⅜ x 8¼. 22895-9 Pa. $4.00

MONOGRAMS AND ALPHABETIC DEVICES, edited by Hayward and Blanche Cirker. Over 2500 combinations, names, crests in very varied styles: script engraving, ornate Victorian, simple Roman, and many others. 226pp. 8⅛ x 11. 22330-2 Pa. $4.00

THE BOOK OF SIGNS, Rudolf Koch. Famed German type designer renders 493 symbols: religious, alchemical, imperial, runes, property marks, etc. Timeless. 104pp. 6⅛ x 9¼. 20162-7 Pa. $1.50

200 DECORATIVE TITLE PAGES, edited by Alexander Nesbitt. 1478 to late 1920's. Baskerville, Dürer, Beardsley, W. Morris, Pyle, many others in most varied techniques. For posters, programs, other uses. 222pp. 8⅜ x 11¼. 21264-5 Pa. $3.50

DICTIONARY OF AMERICAN PORTRAITS, edited by Hayward and Blanche Cirker. 4000 important Americans, earliest times to 1905, mostly in clear line. Politicians, writers, soldiers, scientists, inventors, industrialists, Indians, Blacks, women, outlaws, etc. Identificatory information. 756pp. 9¼ x 12¾. 21823-6 Clothbd. $30.00

ART FORMS IN NATURE, Ernst Haeckel. Multitude of strangely beautiful natural forms: Radiolaria, Foraminifera, jellyfishes, fungi, turtles, bats, etc. All 100 plates of the 19th century evolutionist's Kunstformen der Natur (1904). 100pp. 9⅜ x 12¼. 22987-4 Pa. $4.00

DECOUPAGE: THE BIG PICTURE SOURCEBOOK, Eleanor Rawlings. Make hundreds of beautiful objects, over 550 florals, animals, letters, shells, period costumes, frames, etc. selected by foremost practitioner. Printed on one side of page. 8 color plates. Instructions. 176pp. 9³⁄₁₆ x 12¼. 23182-8 Pa. $5.00

AMERICAN FOLK DECORATION, Jean Lipman, Eve Meulendyke. Thorough coverage of all aspects of wood, tin, leather, paper, cloth decoration — scapes, humans, trees, flowers, geometrics — and how to make them. Full instructions. 233 illustrations, 5 in color. 163pp. 8⅜ x 11¼. 22217-9 Pa. $3.95

WHITTLING AND WOODCARVING, E.J. Tangerman. Best book on market; clear, full. If you can cut a potato, you can carve toys, puzzles, chains, caricatures, masks, patterns, frames, decorate surfaces, etc. Also covers serious wood sculpture. Over 200 photos. 293pp. 20965-2 Pa. $2.50

DRIED FLOWERS, Sarah Whitlock and Martha Rankin. Concise, clear, practical guide to dehydration, glycerinizing, pressing plant material, and more. Covers use of silica gel. 12 drawings. Originally titled "New Techniques with Dried Flowers." 32pp.
21802-3 Pa. $1.00

ABC OF POULTRY RAISING, J.H. Florea. Poultry expert, editor tells how to raise chickens on home or small business basis. Breeds, feeding, housing, laying, etc. Very concrete, practical. 50 illustrations. 256pp.
23201-8 Pa. $3.00

HOW INDIANS USE WILD PLANTS FOR FOOD, MEDICINE & CRAFTS, Frances Densmore. Smithsonian, Bureau of American Ethnology report presents wealth of material on nearly 200 plants used by Chippewas of Minnesota and Wisconsin. 33 plates plus 122pp. of text. 6 1/8 x 9 1/4.
23019-8 Pa. $2.50

THE HERBAL OR GENERAL HISTORY OF PLANTS, John Gerard. The 1633 edition revised and enlarged by Thomas Johnson. Containing almost 2850 plant descriptions and 2705 superb illustrations, Gerard's Herbal is a monumental work, the book all modern English herbals are derived from, and the one herbal every serious enthusiast should have in its entirety. Original editions are worth perhaps $750. 1678pp. 8 1/2 x 12 1/4.
23147-X Clothbd. $50.00

A MODERN HERBAL, Margaret Grieve. Much the fullest, most exact, most useful compilation of herbal material. Gigantic alphabetical encyclopedia, from aconite to zedoary, gives botanical information, medical properties, folklore, economic uses, and much else. Indispensable to serious reader. 161 illustrations. 888pp. 6 1/2 x 9 1/4.
USO 22798-7, 22799-5 Pa., Two vol. set $10.00

HOW TO KNOW THE FERNS, Frances T. Parsons. Delightful classic. Identification, fern lore, for Eastern and Central U.S.A. Has introduced thousands to interesting life form. 99 illustrations. 215pp.
20740-4 Pa. $2.50

THE MUSHROOM HANDBOOK, Louis C.C. Krieger. Still the best popular handbook. Full descriptions of 259 species, extremely thorough text, habitats, luminescence, poisons, folklore, etc. 32 color plates; 126 other illustrations. 560pp.
21861-9 Pa. $4.50

HOW TO KNOW THE WILD FRUITS, Maude G. Peterson. Classic guide covers nearly 200 trees, shrubs, smaller plants of the U.S. arranged by color of fruit and then by family. Full text provides names, descriptions, edibility, uses. 80 illustrations. 400pp.
22943-2 Pa. $3.00

COMMON WEEDS OF THE UNITED STATES, U.S. Department of Agriculture. Covers 220 important weeds with illustration, maps, botanical information, plant lore for each. Over 225 illustrations. 463pp. 6 1/8 x 9 1/4.
20504-5 Pa. $4.50

HOW TO KNOW THE WILD FLOWERS, Mrs. William S. Dana. Still best popular book for East and Central USA. Over 500 plants easily identified, with plant lore; arranged according to color and flowering time. 174 plates. 459pp.
20332-8 Pa. $3.50

EARLY NEW ENGLAND GRAVESTONE RUBBINGS, Edmund V. Gillon, Jr. 43 photographs, 226 rubbings show heavily symbolic, macabre, sometimes humorous primitive American art. Up to early 19th century. 207pp. 8⅜ x 11¼.
21380-3 Pa. $4.00

L.J.M. DAGUERRE: THE HISTORY OF THE DIORAMA AND THE DAGUERREOTYPE, Helmut and Alison Gernsheim. Definitive account. Early history, life and work of Daguerre; discovery of daguerreotype process; diffusion abroad; other early photography. 124 illustrations. 226pp. 6⅙ x 9¼.
22290-X Pa. $4.00

PHOTOGRAPHY AND THE AMERICAN SCENE, Robert Taft. The basic book on American photography as art, recording form, 1839-1889. Development, influence on society, great photographers, types (portraits, war, frontier, etc.), whatever else needed. Inexhaustible. Illustrated with 322 early photos, daguerreotypes, tintypes, stereo slides, etc. 546pp. 6⅛ x 9¼.
21201-7 Pa. $5.00

PHOTOGRAPHIC SKETCHBOOK OF THE CIVIL WAR, Alexander Gardner. Reproduction of 1866 volume with 100 on-the-field photographs: Manassas, Lincoln on battlefield, slave pens, etc. Introduction by E.F. Bleiler. 224pp. 10¾ x 9.
22731-6 Pa. $4.50

THE MOVIES: A PICTURE QUIZ BOOK, Stanley Appelbaum & Hayward Cirker. Match stars with their movies, name actors and actresses, test your movie skill with 241 stills from 236 great movies, 1902-1959. Indexes of performers and films. 128pp. 8⅜ x 9¼.
20222-4 Pa. $2.50

THE TALKIES, Richard Griffith. Anthology of features, articles from Photoplay, 1928-1940, reproduced complete. Stars, famous movies, technical features, fabulous ads, etc.; Garbo, Chaplin, King Kong, Lubitsch, etc. 4 color plates, scores of illustrations. 327pp. 8⅜ x 11¼.
22762-6 Pa. $5.95

THE MOVIE MUSICAL FROM VITAPHONE TO "42ND STREET," edited by Miles Kreuger. Relive the rise of the movie musical as reported in the pages of Photoplay magazine (1926-1933): every movie review, cast list, ad, and record review; every significant feature article, production still, biography, forecast, and gossip story. Profusely illustrated. 367pp. 8⅜ x 11¼.
23154-2 Pa. $6.95

JOHANN SEBASTIAN BACH, Philipp Spitta. Great classic of biography, musical commentary, with hundreds of pieces analyzed. Also good for Bach's contemporaries. 450 musical examples. Total of 1799pp.
EUK 22278-0, 22279-9 Clothbd., Two vol. set $25.00

BEETHOVEN AND HIS NINE SYMPHONIES, Sir George Grove. Thorough history, analysis, commentary on symphonies and some related pieces. For either beginner or advanced student. 436 musical passages. 407pp.
20334-4 Pa. $4.00

MOZART AND HIS PIANO CONCERTOS, Cuthbert Girdlestone. The only full-length study. Detailed analyses of all 21 concertos, sources; 417 musical examples. 509pp.
21271-8 Pa. $4.50

HOUDINI ON MAGIC, Harold Houdini. Edited by Walter Gibson, Morris N. Young. How he escaped; exposés of fake spiritualists; instructions for eye-catching tricks; other fascinating material by and about greatest magician. 155 illustrations. 280pp. 20384-0 Pa. $2.50

HANDBOOK OF THE NUTRITIONAL CONTENTS OF FOOD, U.S. Dept. of Agriculture. Largest, most detailed source of food nutrition information ever prepared. Two mammoth tables: one measuring nutrients in 100 grams of edible portion; the other, in edible portion of 1 pound as purchased. Originally titled Composition of Foods. 190pp. 9 x 12. 21342-0 Pa. $4.00

COMPLETE GUIDE TO HOME CANNING, PRESERVING AND FREEZING, U.S. Dept. of Agriculture. Seven basic manuals with full instructions for jams and jellies; pickles and relishes; canning fruits, vegetables, meat; freezing anything. Really good recipes, exact instructions for optimal results. Save a fortune in food. 156 illustrations. 214pp. 6⅛ x 9¼. 22911-4 Pa. $2.50

THE BREAD TRAY, Louis P. De Gouy. Nearly every bread the cook could buy or make: bread sticks of Italy, fruit breads of Greece, glazed rolls of Vienna, everything from corn pone to croissants. Over 500 recipes altogether. including buns, rolls, muffins, scones, and more. 463pp. 23000-7 Pa. $3.50

CREATIVE HAMBURGER COOKERY, Louis P. De Gouy. 182 unusual recipes for casseroles, meat loaves and hamburgers that turn inexpensive ground meat into memorable main dishes: Arizona chili burgers, burger tamale pie, burger stew, burger corn loaf, burger wine loaf, and more. 120pp. 23001-5 Pa. $1.75

LONG ISLAND SEAFOOD COOKBOOK, J. George Frederick and Jean Joyce. Probably the best American seafood cookbook. Hundreds of recipes. 40 gourmet sauces, 123 recipes using oysters alone! All varieties of fish and seafood amply represented. 324pp. 22677-8 Pa. $3.00

THE EPICUREAN: A COMPLETE TREATISE OF ANALYTICAL AND PRACTICAL STUDIES IN THE CULINARY ART, Charles Ranhofer. Great modern classic. 3,500 recipes from master chef of Delmonico's, turn-of-the-century America's best restaurant. Also explained, many techniques known only to professional chefs. 775 illustrations. 1183pp. 6⅝ x 10. 22680-8 Clothbd. $17.50

THE AMERICAN WINE COOK BOOK, Ted Hatch. Over 700 recipes: old favorites livened up with wine plus many more: Czech fish soup, quince soup, sauce Perigueux, shrimp shortcake, filets Stroganoff, cordon bleu goulash, jambonneau, wine fruit cake, more. 314pp. 22796-0 Pa. $2.50

DELICIOUS VEGETARIAN COOKING, Ivan Baker. Close to 500 delicious and varied recipes: soups, main course dishes (pea, bean, lentil, cheese, vegetable, pasta, and egg dishes), savories, stews, whole-wheat breads and cakes, more. 168pp. USO 22834-7 Pa. $1.75

INCIDENTS OF TRAVEL IN YUCATAN, John L. Stephens. Classic (1843) exploration of jungles of Yucatan, looking for evidences of Maya civilization. Travel adventures, Mexican and Indian culture, etc. Total of 669pp.
20926-1, 20927-X Pa., Two vol. set $5.50

LIVING MY LIFE, Emma Goldman. Candid, no holds barred account by foremost American anarchist: her own life, anarchist movement, famous contemporaries, ideas and their impact. Struggles and confrontations in America, plus deportation to U.S.S.R. Shocking inside account of persecution of anarchists under Lenin. 13 plates. Total of 944pp.
22543-7, 22544-5 Pa., Two vol. set $9.00

AMERICAN INDIANS, George Catlin. Classic account of life among Plains Indians: ceremonies, hunt, warfare, etc. Dover edition reproduces for first time all original paintings. 312 plates. 572pp. of text. 6⅛ x 9¼.
22118-0, 22119-9 Pa., Two vol. set $8.00
22140-7, 22144-X Clothbd., Two vol. set $16.00

THE INDIANS' BOOK, Natalie Curtis. Lore, music, narratives, drawings by Indians, collected from cultures of U.S.A. 149 songs in full notation. 45 illustrations. 583pp. 6⅝ x 9⅜.
21939-9 Pa. $5.00

INDIAN BLANKETS AND THEIR MAKERS, George Wharton James. History, old style wool blankets, changes brought about by traders, symbolism of design and color, a Navajo weaver at work, outline blanket, Kachina blankets, more. Emphasis on Navajo. 130 illustrations, 32 in color. 230pp. 6⅛ x 9¼.
22996-3 Pa. $5.00
23068-6 Clothbd. $10.00

AN INTRODUCTION TO THE STUDY OF THE MAYA HIEROGLYPHS, Sylvanus Griswold Morley. Classic study by one of the truly great figures in hieroglyph research. Still the best introduction for the student for reading Maya hieroglyphs. New introduction by J. Eric S. Thompson. 117 illustrations. 284pp.
23108-9 Pa. $4.00

THE ANALECTS OF CONFUCIUS, THE GREAT LEARNING, DOCTRINE OF THE MEAN, Confucius. Edited by James Legge. Full Chinese text, standard English translation on same page, Chinese commentators, editor's annotations; dictionary of characters at rear, plus grammatical comment. Finest edition anywhere of one of world's greatest thinkers. 503pp.
22746-4 Pa. $4.50

THE I CHING (THE BOOK OF CHANGES), translated by James Legge. Complete translation of basic text plus appendices by Confucius, and Chinese commentary of most penetrating divination manual ever prepared. Indispensable to study of early Oriental civilizations, to modern inquiring reader. 448pp.
21062-6 Pa. $3.50

THE EGYPTIAN BOOK OF THE DEAD, E.A. Wallis Budge. Complete reproduction of Ani's papyrus, finest ever found. Full hieroglyphic text, interlinear transliteration, word for word translation, smooth translation. Basic work, for Egyptology, for modern study of psychic matters. Total of 533pp. 6½ x 9¼.
EBE 21866-X Pa. $4.95

JEWISH GREETING CARDS, Ed Sibbett, Jr. 16 cards to cut and color. Three say "Happy Chanukah," one "Happy New Year," others have no message, show stars of David, Torahs, wine cups, other traditional themes. 16 envelopes. 8¼ x 11.
23225-5 Pa. $2.00

AUBREY BEARDSLEY GREETING CARD BOOK, Aubrey Beardsley. Edited by Theodore Menten. 16 elegant yet inexpensive greeting cards let you combine your own sentiments with subtle Art Nouveau lines. 16 different Aubrey Beardsley designs that you can color or not, as you wish. 16 envelopes. 64pp. 8¼ x 11.
23173-9 Pa. $2.00

RECREATIONS IN THE THEORY OF NUMBERS, Albert Beiler. Number theory, an inexhaustible source of puzzles, recreations, for beginners and advanced. Divisors, perfect numbers. scales of notation, etc. 349pp.
21096-0 Pa. $2.50

AMUSEMENTS IN MATHEMATICS, Henry E. Dudeney. One of largest puzzle collections, based on algebra, arithmetic, permutations, probability, plane figure dissection, properties of numbers, by one of world's foremost puzzlists. Solutions. 450 illustrations. 258pp.
20473-1 Pa. $2.75

MATHEMATICS, MAGIC AND MYSTERY, Martin Gardner. Puzzle editor for Scientific American explains math behind: card tricks, stage mind reading, coin and match tricks, counting out games, geometric dissections. Probability, sets, theory of numbers, clearly explained. Plus more than 400 tricks, guaranteed to work. 135 illustrations. 176pp.
20335-2 Pa. $2.00

BEST MATHEMATICAL PUZZLES OF SAM LOYD, edited by Martin Gardner. Bizarre, original, whimsical puzzles by America's greatest puzzler. From fabulously rare Cyclopedia, including famous 14-15 puzzles, the Horse of a Different Color, 115 more. Elementary math. 150 illustrations. 167pp.
20498-7 Pa. $2.00

MATHEMATICAL PUZZLES FOR BEGINNERS AND ENTHUSIASTS, Geoffrey Mott-Smith. 189 puzzles from easy to difficult involving arithmetic, logic, algebra, properties of digits, probability. Explanation of math behind puzzles. 135 illustrations. 248pp.
20198-8 Pa. $2.00

BIG BOOK OF MAZES AND LABYRINTHS, Walter Shepherd. Classical, solid, and ripple mazes; short path and avoidance labyrinths; more —50 mazes and labyrinths in all. 12 other figures. Full solutions. 112pp. 8⅛ x 11.
22951-3 Pa. $2.00

COIN GAMES AND PUZZLES, Maxey Brooke. 60 puzzles, games and stunts — from Japan, Korea, Africa and the ancient world, by Dudeney and the other great puzzlers, as well as Maxey Brooke's own creations. Full solutions. 67 illustrations. 94pp.
22893-2 Pa. $1.25

HAND SHADOWS TO BE THROWN UPON THE WALL, Henry Bursill. Wonderful Victorian novelty tells how to make flying birds, dog, goose, deer, and 14 others. 32pp. 6½ x 9¼.
21779-5 Pa. $1.00

MANUAL OF THE TREES OF NORTH AMERICA, Charles S. Sargent. The basic survey of every native tree and tree-like shrub, 717 species in all. Extremely full descriptions, information on habitat, growth, locales, economics, etc. Necessary to every serious tree lover. Over 100 finding keys. 783 illustrations. Total of 986pp.
20277-1, 20278-X Pa., Two vol. set $8.00

BIRDS OF THE NEW YORK AREA, John Bull. Indispensable guide to more than 400 species within a hundred-mile radius of Manhattan. Information on range, status, breeding, migration, distribution trends, etc. Foreword by Roger Tory Peterson. 17 drawings; maps. 540pp.
23222-0 Pa. $6.00

THE SEA-BEACH AT EBB-TIDE, Augusta Foote Arnold. Identify hundreds of marine plants and animals: algae, seaweeds, squids, crabs, corals, etc. Descriptions cover food, life cycle, size, shape, habitat. Over 600 drawings. 490pp.
21949-6 Pa. $4.00

THE MOTH BOOK, William J. Holland. Identify more than 2,000 moths of North America. General information, precise species descriptions. 623 illustrations plus 48 color plates show almost all species, full size. 1968 edition. Still the basic book. Total of 551pp. 6½ x 9¼.
21948-8 Pa. $6.00

AN INTRODUCTION TO THE REPTILES AND AMPHIBIANS OF THE UNITED STATES, Percy A. Morris. All lizards, crocodiles, turtles, snakes, toads, frogs; life history, identification, habits, suitability as pets, etc. Non-technical, but sound and broad. 130 photos. 253pp.
22982-3 Pa. $3.00

OLD NEW YORK IN EARLY PHOTOGRAPHS, edited by Mary Black. Your only chance to see New York City as it was 1853-1906, through 196 wonderful photographs from N.Y. Historical Society. Great Blizzard, Lincoln's funeral procession, great buildings. 228pp. 9 x 12.
22907-6 Pa. $6.00

THE AMERICAN REVOLUTION, A PICTURE SOURCEBOOK, John Grafton. Wonderful Bicentennial picture source, with 411 illustrations (contemporary and 19th century) showing battles, personalities, maps, events, flags, posters, soldier's life, ships, etc. all captioned and explained. A wonderful browsing book, supplement to other historical reading. 160pp. 9 x 12.
23226-3 Pa. $4.00

PERSONAL NARRATIVE OF A PILGRIMAGE TO AL-MADINAH AND MECCAH, Richard Burton. Great travel classic by remarkably colorful personality. Burton, disguised as a Moroccan, visited sacred shrines of Islam, narrowly escaping death. Wonderful observations of Islamic life, customs, personalities. 47 illustrations. Total of 959pp.
21217-3, 21218-1 Pa., Two vol. set $7.00

INCIDENTS OF TRAVEL IN CENTRAL AMERICA, CHIAPAS, AND YUCATAN, John L. Stephens. Almost single-handed discovery of Maya culture; exploration of ruined cities, monuments, temples; customs of Indians. 115 drawings. 892pp.
22404-X, 22405-8 Pa., Two vol. set $8.00

MODERN CHESS STRATEGY, Ludek Pachman. The use of the queen, the active king, exchanges, pawn play, the center, weak squares, etc. Section on rook alone worth price of the book. Stress on the moderns. Often considered the most important book on strategy. 314pp. 20290-9 Pa. $3.00

CHESS STRATEGY, Edward Lasker. One of half-dozen great theoretical works in chess, shows principles of action above and beyond moves. Acclaimed by Capablanca, Keres, etc. 282pp. USO 20528-2 Pa. $2.50

CHESS PRAXIS, THE PRAXIS OF MY SYSTEM, Aron Nimzovich. Founder of hypermodern chess explains his profound, influential theories that have dominated much of 20th century chess. 109 illustrative games. 369pp. 20296-8 Pa. $3.50

HOW TO PLAY THE CHESS OPENINGS, Eugene Znosko-Borovsky. Clear, profound examinations of just what each opening is intended to do and how opponent can counter. Many sample games, questions and answers. 147pp. 22795-2 Pa. $2.00

THE ART OF CHESS COMBINATION, Eugene Znosko-Borovsky. Modern explanation of principles, varieties, techniques and ideas behind them, illustrated with many examples from great players. 212pp. 20583-5 Pa. $2.00

COMBINATIONS: THE HEART OF CHESS, Irving Chernev. Step-by-step explanation of intricacies of combinative play. 356 combinations by Tarrasch, Botvinnik, Keres, Steinitz, Anderssen, Morphy, Marshall, Capablanca, others, all annotated. 245 pp. 21744-2 Pa. $2.50

HOW TO PLAY CHESS ENDINGS, Eugene Znosko-Borovsky. Thorough instruction manual by fine teacher analyzes each piece individually; many common endgame situations. Examines games by Steinitz, Alekhine, Lasker, others. Emphasis on understanding. 288pp. 21170-3 Pa. $2.75

MORPHY'S GAMES OF CHESS, Philip W. Sergeant. Romantic history, 54 games of greatest player of all time against Anderssen, Bird, Paulsen, Harrwitz; 52 games at odds; 52 blindfold; 100 consultation, informal, other games. Analyses by Anderssen, Steinitz, Morphy himself. 352pp. 20386-7 Pa. $2.75

500 MASTER GAMES OF CHESS, S. Tartakower, J. du Mont. Vast collection of great chess games from 1798-1938, with much material nowhere else readily available. Fully annotated, arranged by opening for easier study. 665pp. 23208-5 Pa. $6.00

THE SOVIET SCHOOL OF CHESS, Alexander Kotov and M. Yudovich. Authoritative work on modern Russian chess. History, conceptual background. 128 fully annotated games (most unavailable elsewhere) by Botvinnik, Keres, Smyslov, Tal, Petrosian, Spassky, more. 390pp. 20026-4 Pa. $3.95

WONDERS AND CURIOSITIES OF CHESS, Irving Chernev. A lifetime's accumulation of such wonders and curiosities as the longest won game, shortest game, chess problem with mate in 1220 moves, and much more unusual material — 356 items in all, over 160 complete games. 146 diagrams. 203pp. 23007-4 Pa. $3.50

MOTHER GOOSE'S MELODIES. Facsimile of fabulously rare Munroe and Francis "copyright 1833" Boston edition. Familiar and unusual rhymes, wonderful old woodcut illustrations. Edited by E.F. Bleiler. 128pp. 4½ x 6⅜. 22577-1 Pa. $1.00

MOTHER GOOSE IN HIEROGLYPHICS. Favorite nursery rhymes presented in rebus form for children. Fascinating 1849 edition reproduced in toto, with key. Introduction by E.F. Bleiler. About 400 woodcuts. 64pp. 6⅞ x 5¼. 20745-5 Pa. $1.00

PETER PIPER'S PRACTICAL PRINCIPLES OF PLAIN & PERFECT PRONUNCIATION. Alliterative jingles and tongue-twisters. Reproduction in full of 1830 first American edition. 25 spirited woodcuts. 32pp. 4½ x 6⅜. 22560-7 Pa. $1.00

MARMADUKE MULTIPLY'S MERRY METHOD OF MAKING MINOR MATHEMATICIANS. Fellow to Peter Piper, it teaches multiplication table by catchy rhymes and woodcuts. 1841 Munroe & Francis edition. Edited by E.F. Bleiler. 103pp. 4⅝ x 6.
22773-1 Pa. $1.25
20171-6 Clothbd. $3.00

THE NIGHT BEFORE CHRISTMAS, Clement Moore. Full text, and woodcuts from original 1848 book. Also critical, historical material. 19 illustrations. 40pp. 4⅝ x 6. 22797-9 Pa. $1.00

THE KING OF THE GOLDEN RIVER, John Ruskin. Victorian children's classic of three brothers, their attempts to reach the Golden River, what becomes of them. Facsimile of original 1889 edition. 22 illustrations. 56pp. 4⅝ x 6⅜.
20066-3 Pa. $1.25

DREAMS OF THE RAREBIT FIEND, Winsor McCay. Pioneer cartoon strip, unexcelled for beauty, imagination, in 60 full sequences. Incredible technical virtuosity, wonderful visual wit. Historical introduction. 62pp. 8⅜ x 11¼. 21347-1 Pa. $2.00

THE KATZENJAMMER KIDS, Rudolf Dirks. In full color, 14 strips from 1906-7; full of imagination, characteristic humor. Classic of great historical importance. Introduction by August Derleth. 32pp. 9¼ x 12¼. 23005-8 Pa. $2.00

LITTLE ORPHAN ANNIE AND LITTLE ORPHAN ANNIE IN COSMIC CITY, Harold Gray. Two great sequences from the early strips: our curly-haired heroine defends the Warbucks' financial empire and, then, takes on meanie Phineas P. Pinchpenny. Leapin' lizards! 178pp. 6⅛ x 8⅜. 23107-0 Pa. $2.00

WHEN A FELLER NEEDS A FRIEND, Clare Briggs. 122 cartoons by one of the greatest newspaper cartoonists of the early 20th century — about growing up, making a living, family life, daily frustrations and occasional triumphs. 121pp. 8½ x 9½.
23148-8 Pa. $2.50

THE BEST OF GLUYAS WILLIAMS. 100 drawings by one of America's finest cartoonists: The Day a Cake of Ivory Soap Sank at Proctor & Gamble's, At the Life Insurance Agents' Banquet, and many other gems from the 20's and 30's. 118pp. 8⅜ x 11¼. 22737-5 Pa. $2.50

SLEEPING BEAUTY, illustrated by Arthur Rackham. Perhaps the fullest, most delightful version ever, told by C.S. Evans. Rackham's best work. 49 illustrations. 110pp. 7⅞ x 10¾. 22756-1 Pa. $2.00

THE WONDERFUL WIZARD OF OZ, L. Frank Baum. Facsimile in full color of America's finest children's classic. Introduction by Martin Gardner. 143 illustrations by W.W. Denslow. 267pp. 20691-2 Pa. $2.50

GOOPS AND HOW TO BE THEM, Gelett Burgess. Classic tongue-in-cheek masquerading as etiquette book. 87 verses, 170 cartoons as Goops demonstrate virtues of table manners, neatness, courtesy, more. 88pp. 6½ x 9¼. 22233-0 Pa. $1.50

THE BROWNIES, THEIR BOOK, Palmer Cox. Small as mice, cunning as foxes, exuberant, mischievous, Brownies go to zoo, toy shop, seashore, circus, more. 24 verse adventures. 266 illustrations. 144pp. 6⅝ x 9¼. 21265-3 Pa. $1.75

BILLY WHISKERS: THE AUTOBIOGRAPHY OF A GOAT, Frances Trego Montgomery. Escapades of that rambunctious goat. Favorite from turn of the century America. 24 illustrations. 259pp. 22345-0 Pa. $2.75

THE ROCKET BOOK, Peter Newell. Fritz, janitor's kid, sets off rocket in basement of apartment house; an ingenious hole punched through every page traces course of rocket. 22 duotone drawings, verses. 48pp. 6⅞ x 8⅜. 22044-3 Pa. $1.50

PECK'S BAD BOY AND HIS PA, George W. Peck. Complete double-volume of great American childhood classic. Hennery's ingenious pranks against outraged pomposity of pa and the grocery man. 97 illustrations. Introduction by E.F. Bleiler. 347pp. 20497-9 Pa. $2.50

THE TALE OF PETER RABBIT, Beatrix Potter. The inimitable Peter's terrifying adventure in Mr. McGregor's garden, with all 27 wonderful, full-color Potter illustrations. 55pp. 4¼ x 5½. USO 22827-4 Pa. $1.00

THE TALE OF MRS. TIGGY-WINKLE, Beatrix Potter. Your child will love this story about a very special hedgehog and all 27 wonderful, full-color Potter illustrations. 57pp. 4¼ x 5½. USO 20546-0 Pa. $1.00

THE TALE OF BENJAMIN BUNNY, Beatrix Potter. Peter Rabbit's cousin coaxes him back into Mr. McGregor's garden for a whole new set of adventures. A favorite with children. All 27 full-color illustrations. 59pp. 4¼ x 5½. USO 21102-9 Pa. $1.00

THE MERRY ADVENTURES OF ROBIN HOOD, Howard Pyle. Facsimile of original (1883) edition, finest modern version of English outlaw's adventures. 23 illustrations by Pyle. 296pp. 6½ x 9¼. 22043-5 Pa. $2.75

TWO LITTLE SAVAGES, Ernest Thompson Seton. Adventures of two boys who lived as Indians; explaining Indian ways, woodlore, pioneer methods. 293 illustrations. 286pp. 20985-7 Pa. $3.00

# CATALOGUE OF DOVER BOOKS

THE ART DECO STYLE, ed. by Theodore Menten. Furniture, jewelry, metalwork, ceramics, fabrics, lighting fixtures, interior decors, exteriors, graphics from pure French sources. Best sampling around. Over 400 photographs. 183pp. 8⅜ x 11¼.
22824-X Pa. $4.00

THE GENTLEMAN AND CABINET MAKER'S DIRECTOR, Thomas Chippendale. Full reprint, 1762 style book, most influential of all time; chairs, tables, sofas, mirrors, cabinets, etc. 200 plates, plus 24 photographs of surviving pieces. 249pp. 9⅞ x 12¾.
21601-2 Pa. $5.00

PINE FURNITURE OF EARLY NEW ENGLAND, Russell H. Kettell. Basic book. Thorough historical text, plus 200 illustrations of boxes, highboys, candlesticks, desks, etc. 477pp. 7⅞ x 10¾.
20145-7 Clothbd. $12.50

ORIENTAL RUGS, ANTIQUE AND MODERN, Walter A. Hawley. Persia, Turkey, Caucasus, Central Asia, China, other traditions. Best general survey of all aspects: styles and periods, manufacture, uses, symbols and their interpretation, and identification. 96 illustrations, 11 in color. 320pp. 6⅛ x 9¼.
22366-3 Pa. $5.00

DECORATIVE ANTIQUE IRONWORK, Henry R. d'Allemagne. Photographs of 4500 iron artifacts from world's finest collection, Rouen. Hinges, locks, candelabra, weapons, lighting devices, clocks, tools, from Roman times to mid-19th century. Nothing else comparable to it. 420pp. 9 x 12.
22082-6 Pa. $8.50

THE COMPLETE BOOK OF DOLL MAKING AND COLLECTING, Catherine Christopher. Instructions, patterns for dozens of dolls, from rag doll on up to elaborate, historically accurate figures. Mould faces, sew clothing, make doll houses, etc. Also collecting information. Many illustrations. 288pp. 6 x 9. 22066-4 Pa. $3.00

ANTIQUE PAPER DOLLS: 1915-1920, edited by Arnold Arnold. 7 antique cut-out dolls and 24 costumes from 1915-1920, selected by Arnold Arnold from his collection of rare children's books and entertainments, all in full color. 32pp. 9¼ x 12¼.
23176-3 Pa. $2.00

ANTIQUE PAPER DOLLS: THE EDWARDIAN ERA, Epinal. Full-color reproductions of two historic series of paper dolls that show clothing styles in 1908 and at the beginning of the First World War. 8 two-sided, stand-up dolls and 32 complete, two-sided costumes. Full instructions for assembling included. 32pp. 9¼ x 12¼.
23175-5 Pa. $2.00

A HISTORY OF COSTUME, Carl Köhler, Emma von Sichardt. Egypt, Babylon, Greece up through 19th century Europe; based on surviving pieces, art works, etc. Full text and 595 illustrations, including many clear, measured patterns for reproducing historic costume. Practical. 464pp. 21030-8 Pa. $4.00

EARLY AMERICAN LOCOMOTIVES, John H. White, Jr. Finest locomotive engravings from late 19th century: historical (1804-1874), main-line (after 1870), special, foreign, etc. 147 plates. 200pp. 11⅜ x 8¼. 22772-3 Pa. $3.50

THE BEST DR. THORNDYKE DETECTIVE STORIES, R. Austin Freeman. The Case of Oscar Brodski, The Moabite Cipher, and 5 other favorites featuring the great scientific detective, plus his long-believed-lost first adventure — 31 New Inn — reprinted here for the first time. Edited by E.F. Bleiler. USO 20388-3 Pa. $3.00

BEST "THINKING MACHINE" DETECTIVE STORIES, Jacques Futrelle. The Problem of Cell 13 and 11 other stories about Prof. Augustus S.F.X. Van Dusen, including two "lost" stories. First reprinting of several. Edited by E.F. Bleiler. 241pp.
20537-1 Pa. $3.00

UNCLE SILAS, J. Sheridan LeFanu. Victorian Gothic mystery novel, considered by many best of period, even better than Collins or Dickens. Wonderful psychological terror. Introduction by Frederick Shroyer. 436pp. 21715-9 Pa. $4.00

BEST DR. POGGIOLI DETECTIVE STORIES, T.S. Stribling. 15 best stories from EQMM and The Saint offer new adventures in Mexico, Florida, Tennessee hills as Poggioli unravels mysteries and combats Count Jalacki. 217pp. 23227-1 Pa. $3.00

EIGHT DIME NOVELS, selected with an introduction by E.F. Bleiler. Adventures of Old King Brady, Frank James, Nick Carter, Deadwood Dick, Buffalo Bill, The Steam Man, Frank Merriwell, and Horatio Alger — 1877 to 1905. Important, entertaining popular literature in facsimile reprint, with original covers. 190pp. 9 x 12.
22975-0 Pa. $3.50

ALICE'S ADVENTURES UNDER GROUND, Lewis Carroll. Facsimile of ms. Carroll gave Alice Liddell in 1864. Different in many ways from final Alice. Handlettered, illustrated by Carroll. Introduction by Martin Gardner. 128pp. 21482-6 Pa. $1.50

ALICE IN WONDERLAND COLORING BOOK, Lewis Carroll. Pictures by John Tenniel. Large-size versions of the famous illustrations of Alice, Cheshire Cat, Mad Hatter and all the others, waiting for your crayons. Abridged text. 36 illustrations. 64pp. 8¼ x 11.
22853-3 Pa. $1.50

AVENTURES D'ALICE AU PAYS DES MERVEILLES, Lewis Carroll. Bué's translation of "Alice" into French, supervised by Carroll himself. Novel way to learn language. (No English text.) 42 Tenniel illustrations. 196pp. 22836-3 Pa. $2.00

MYTHS AND FOLK TALES OF IRELAND, Jeremiah Curtin. 11 stories that are Irish versions of European fairy tales and 9 stories from the Fenian cycle — 20 tales of legend and magic that comprise an essential work in the history of folklore. 256pp.
22430-9 Pa. $3.00

EAST O' THE SUN AND WEST O' THE MOON, George W. Dasent. Only full edition of favorite, wonderful Norwegian fairytales — Why the Sea is Salt, Boots and the Troll, etc. — with 77 illustrations by Kittelsen & Werenskiöld. 418pp.
22521-6 Pa. $3.50

PERRAULT'S FAIRY TALES, Charles Perrault and Gustave Doré. Original versions of Cinderella, Sleeping Beauty, Little Red Riding Hood, etc. in best translation, with 34 wonderful illustrations by Gustave Doré. 117pp. 8⅛ x 11. 22311-6 Pa. $2.50

THE JOURNAL OF HENRY D. THOREAU, edited by Bradford Torrey, F.H. Allen. Complete reprinting of 14 volumes, 1837-1861, over two million words; the sourcebooks for Walden, etc. Definitive. All original sketches, plus 75 photographs. Introduction by Walter Harding. Total of 1804pp. 8½ x 12¼.
20312-3, 20313-1 Clothbd., Two vol. set $50.00

MASTERS OF THE DRAMA, John Gassner. Most comprehensive history of the drama, every tradition from Greeks to modern Europe and America, including Orient. Covers 800 dramatists, 2000 plays; biography, plot summaries, criticism, theatre history, etc. 77 illustrations. 890pp. 20100-7 Clothbd. $10.00

GHOST AND HORROR STORIES OF AMBROSE BIERCE, Ambrose Bierce. 23 modern horror stories: The Eyes of the Panther, The Damned Thing, etc., plus the dreamessay Visions of the Night. Edited by E.F. Bleiler. 199pp. 20767-6 Pa. $2.00

BEST GHOST STORIES, Algernon Blackwood. 13 great stories by foremost British 20th century supernaturalist. The Willows, The Wendigo, Ancient Sorceries, others. Edited by E.F. Bleiler. 366pp. USO 22977-7 Pa. $3.00

THE BEST TALES OF HOFFMANN, E.T.A. Hoffmann. 10 of Hoffmann's most important stories, in modern re-editings of standard translations: Nutcracker and the King of Mice, The Golden Flowerpot, etc. 7 illustrations by Hoffmann. Edited by E.F. Bleiler. 458pp. 21793-0 Pa. $3.95

BEST GHOST STORIES OF J.S. LEFANU, J. Sheridan LeFanu. 16 stories by greatest Victorian master: Green Tea, Carmilla, Haunted Baronet, The Familiar, etc. Mostly unavailable elsewhere. Edited by E.F. Bleiler. 8 illustrations. 467pp.
20415-4 Pa. $4.00

SUPERNATURAL HORROR IN LITERATURE, H.P. Lovecraft. Great modern American supernaturalist brilliantly surveys history of genre to 1930's, summarizing, evaluating scores of books. Necessary for every student, lover of form. Introduction by E.F. Bleiler. 111pp. 20105-8 Pa. $1.50

THREE GOTHIC NOVELS, ed. by E.F. Bleiler. Full texts Castle of Otranto, Walpole; Vathek, Beckford; The Vampyre, Polidori; Fragment of a Novel, Lord Byron. 331pp. 21232-7 Pa. $3.00

SEVEN SCIENCE FICTION NOVELS, H.G. Wells. Full novels. First Men in the Moon, Island of Dr. Moreau, War of the Worlds, Food of the Gods, Invisible Man, Time Machine, In the Days of the Comet. A basic science-fiction library. 1015pp.
USO 20264-X Clothbd. $6.00

LADY AUDLEY'S SECRET, Mary E. Braddon. Great Victorian mystery classic, beautifully plotted, suspenseful; praised by Thackeray, Boucher, Starrett, others. What happened to beautiful, vicious Lady Audley's husband? Introduction by Norman Donaldson. 286pp. 23011-2 Pa. $3.00

THE MAGIC MOVING PICTURE BOOK, Bliss, Sands & Co. The pictures in this book move! Volcanoes erupt, a house burns, a serpentine dancer wiggles her way through a number. By using a specially ruled acetate screen provided, you can obtain these and 15 other startling effects. Originally "The Motograph Moving Picture Book." 32pp. 8¼ x 11.                23224-7 Pa. $1.75

STRING FIGURES AND HOW TO MAKE THEM, Caroline F. Jayne. Fullest, clearest instructions on string figures from around world: Eskimo, Navajo, Lapp, Europe, more. Cats cradle, moving spear, lightning, stars. Introduction by A.C. Haddon. 950 illustrations. 407pp.                20152-X Pa. $3.00

PAPER FOLDING FOR BEGINNERS, William D. Murray and Francis J. Rigney. Clearest book on market for making origami sail boats, roosters, frogs that move legs, cups, bonbon boxes. 40 projects. More than 275 illustrations. Photographs. 94pp.
20713-7 Pa. $1.25

INDIAN SIGN LANGUAGE, William Tomkins. Over 525 signs developed by Sioux, Blackfoot, Cheyenne, Arapahoe and other tribes. Written instructions and diagrams: how to make words, construct sentences. Also 290 pictographs of Sioux and Ojibway tribes. 111pp. 6⅛ x 9¼.                22029-X Pa. $1.50

BOOMERANGS: HOW TO MAKE AND THROW THEM, Bernard S. Mason. Easy to make and throw, dozens of designs: cross-stick, pinwheel, boomabird, tumblestick, Australian curved stick boomerang. Complete throwing instructions. All safe. 99pp.                23028-7 Pa. $1.50

25 KITES THAT FLY, Leslie Hunt. Full, easy to follow instructions for kites made from inexpensive materials. Many novelties. Reeling, raising, designing your own. 70 illustrations. 110pp.                22550-X Pa. $1.25

TRICKS AND GAMES ON THE POOL TABLE, Fred Herrmann. 79 tricks and games, some solitaires, some for 2 or more players, some competitive; mystifying shots and throws, unusual carom, tricks involving cork, coins, a hat, more. 77 figures. 95pp.                21814-7 Pa. $1.25

WOODCRAFT AND CAMPING, Bernard S. Mason. How to make a quick emergency shelter, select woods that will burn immediately, make do with limited supplies, etc. Also making many things out of wood, rawhide, bark, at camp. Formerly titled Woodcraft. 295 illustrations. 580pp.                21951-8 Pa. $4.00

AN INTRODUCTION TO CHESS MOVES AND TACTICS SIMPLY EXPLAINED, Leonard Barden. Informal intermediate introduction: reasons for moves, tactics, openings, traps, positional play, endgame. Isolates patterns. 102pp. USO 21210-6 Pa. $1.35

LASKER'S MANUAL OF CHESS, Dr. Emanuel Lasker. Great world champion offers very thorough coverage of all aspects of chess. Combinations, position play, openings, endgame, aesthetics of chess, philosophy of struggle, much more. Filled with analyzed games. 390pp.                20640-8 Pa. $3.50

THE STYLE OF PALESTRINA AND THE DISSONANCE, Knud Jeppesen. Standard analysis of rhythm, line, harmony, accented and unaccented dissonances. Also pre-Palestrina dissonances. 306pp. 22386-8 Pa. $3.00

DOVER OPERA GUIDE AND LIBRETTO SERIES prepared by Ellen H. Bleiler. Each volume contains everything needed for background, complete enjoyment: complete libretto, new English translation with all repeats, biography of composer and librettist, early performance history, musical lore, much else. All volumes lavishly illustrated with performance photos, portraits, similar material. Do not confuse with skimpy performance booklets.

CARMEN, Georges Bizet. 66 illustrations. 222pp. 22111-3 Pa. $2.00

DON GIOVANNI, Wolfgang A. Mozart. 92 illustrations. 209pp. 21134-7 Pa. $2.50

LA BOHÈME, Giacomo Puccini. 73 illustrations. 124pp. USO 20404-9 Pa. $1.75

ÄIDA, Giuseppe Verdi. 76 illustrations. 181pp. 20405-7 Pa. $2.00

LUCIA DI LAMMERMOOR, Gaetano Donizetti. 44 illustrations. 186pp. 22110-5 Pa. $2.00

ANTONIO STRADIVARI: HIS LIFE AND WORK, W. H. Hill, et al. Great work of musicology. Construction methods, woods, varnishes, known instruments, types of instruments, life, special features. Introduction by Sydney Beck. 98 illustrations, plus 4 color plates. 315pp. 20425-1 Pa. $3.00

MUSIC FOR THE PIANO, James Friskin, Irwin Freundlich. Both famous, little-known compositions; 1500 to 1950's. Listing, description, classification, technical aspects for student, teacher, performer. Indispensable for enlarging repertory. 448pp. 22918-1 Pa. $4.00

PIANOS AND THEIR MAKERS, Alfred Dolge. Leading inventor offers full history of piano technology, earliest models to 1910. Types, makers, components, mechanisms, musical aspects. Very strong on offtrail models, inventions; also player pianos. 300 illustrations. 581pp. 22856-8 Pa. $5.00

KEYBOARD MUSIC, J.S. Bach. Bach-Gesellschaft edition. For harpsichord, piano, other keyboard instruments. English Suites, French Suites, Six Partitas, Goldberg Variations, Two-Part Inventions, Three-Part Sinfonias. 312pp. 8⅛ x 11. 22360-4 Pa. $5.00

COMPLETE STRING QUARTETS, Ludwig van Beethoven. Breitkopf and Härtel edition. 6 quartets of Opus 18; 3 quartets of Opus 59; Opera 74, 95, 127, 130, 131, 132, 135 and Grosse Fuge. Study score. 434pp. 9⅜ x 12¼. 22361-2 Pa. $7.95

COMPLETE PIANO SONATAS AND VARIATIONS FOR SOLO PIANO, Johannes Brahms. All sonatas, five variations on themes from Schumann, Paganini, Handel, etc. Vienna Gesellschaft der Musikfreunde edition. 178pp. 9 x 12. 22650-6 Pa. $4.00

PIANO MUSIC 1888-1905, Claude Debussy. Deux Arabesques, Suite Bergamesque, Masques, 1st series of Images, etc. 9 others, in corrected editions. 175pp. 9⅜ x 12¼. 22771-5 Pa. $4.00

VICTORIAN HOUSES: A TREASURY OF LESSER-KNOWN EXAMPLES, Edmund Gillon and Clay Lancaster. 116 photographs, excellent commentary illustrate distinct characteristics, many borrowings of local Victorian architecture. Octagonal houses, Americanized chalets, grand country estates, small cottages, etc. Rich heritage often overlooked. 116 plates. 11⅜ x 10. 22966-1 Pa. $4.00

STICKS AND STONES, Lewis Mumford. Great classic of American cultural history; architecture from medieval-inspired earliest forms to 20th century; evolution of structure and style, influence of environment. 21 illustrations. 113pp. 20202-X Pa. $2.00

ON THE LAWS OF JAPANESE PAINTING, Henry P. Bowie. Best substitute for training with genius Oriental master, based on years of study in Kano school. Philosophy, brushes, inks, style, etc. 66 illustrations. 117pp. 6⅛ x 9¼. 20030-2 Pa. $4.00

A HANDBOOK OF ANATOMY FOR ART STUDENTS, Arthur Thomson. Virtually exhaustive. Skeletal structure, muscles, heads, special features. Full text, anatomical figures, undraped photos. Male and female. 337 illustrations. 459pp. 21163-0 Pa. $5.00

AN ATLAS OF ANATOMY FOR ARTISTS, Fritz Schider. Finest text, working book. Full text, plus anatomical illustrations; plates by great artists showing anatomy. 593 illustrations. 192pp. 7⅞ x 10¾. 20241-0 Clothbd. $6.95

THE HUMAN FIGURE IN MOTION, Eadweard Muybridge. More than 4500 stopped-action photos, in action series, showing undraped men, women, children jumping, lying down, throwing, sitting, wrestling, carrying, etc. "Unparalleled dictionary for artists," American Artist. Taken by great 19th century photographer. 390pp. 7⅞ x 10⅝. 20204-6 Clothbd. $12.50

AN ATLAS OF ANIMAL ANATOMY FOR ARTISTS, W. Ellenberger et al. Horses, dogs, cats, lions, cattle, deer, etc. Muscles, skeleton, surface features. The basic work. Enlarged edition. 288 illustrations. 151pp. 9⅜ x 12¼. 20082-5 Pa. $4.00

LETTER FORMS: 110 COMPLETE ALPHABETS, Frederick Lambert. 110 sets of capital letters; 16 lower case alphabets; 70 sets of numbers and other symbols. Edited and expanded by Theodore Menten. 110pp. 8⅛ x 11. 22872-X Pa. $2.50

THE METHODS OF CONSTRUCTION OF CELTIC ART, George Bain. Simple geometric techniques for making wonderful Celtic interlacements, spirals, Kells-type initials, animals, humans, etc. Unique for artists, craftsmen. Over 500 illustrations. 160pp. 9 x 12. USO 22923-8 Pa. $4.00

SCULPTURE, PRINCIPLES AND PRACTICE, Louis Slobodkin. Step by step approach to clay, plaster, metals, stone; classical and modern. 253 drawings, photos. 255pp. 8⅛ x 11. 22960-2 Pa. $4.50

THE ART OF ETCHING, E.S. Lumsden. Clear, detailed instructions for etching, drypoint, softground, aquatint; from 1st sketch to print. Very detailed, thorough. 200 illustrations. 376pp. 20049-3 Pa. $3.50

EGYPTIAN MAGIC, E.A. Wallis Budge. Foremost Egyptologist, curator at British Museum, on charms, curses, amulets, doll magic, transformations, control of demons, deific appearances, feats of great magicians. Many texts cited. 19 illustrations. 234pp.                                                         USO 22681-6 Pa. $2.50

THE LEYDEN PAPYRUS: AN EGYPTIAN MAGICAL BOOK, edited by F. Ll. Griffith, Herbert Thompson. Egyptian sorcerer's manual contains scores of spells: sex magic of various sorts, occult information, evoking visions, removing evil magic, etc. Transliteration faces translation. 207pp.                         22994-7 Pa. $2.50

THE MALLEUS MALEFICARUM OF KRAMER AND SPRENGER, translated, edited by Montague Summers. Full text of most important witchhunter's "Bible," used by both Catholics and Protestants. Theory of witches, manifestations, remedies, etc. Indispensable to serious student. 278pp. 6⅝ x 10.             USO 22802-9 Pa. $3.95

LOST CONTINENTS, L. Sprague de Camp. Great science-fiction author, finest, fullest study: Atlantis, Lemuria, Mu, Hyperborea, etc. Lost Tribes, Irish in pre-Columbian America, root races; in history, literature, art, occultism. Necessary to everyone concerned with theme. 17 illustrations. 348pp.        22668-9 Pa. $3.50

THE COMPLETE BOOKS OF CHARLES FORT, Charles Fort. Book of the Damned, Lo!, Wild Talents, New Lands. Greatest compilation of data: celestial appearances, flying saucers, falls of frogs, strange disappearances, inexplicable data not recognized by science. Inexhaustible, painstakingly documented. Do not confuse with modern charlatanry. Introduction by Damon Knight. Total of 1126pp.
23094-5 Clothbd. $15.00

FADS AND FALLACIES IN THE NAME OF SCIENCE, Martin Gardner. Fair, witty appraisal of cranks and quacks of science: Atlantis, Lemuria, flat earth, Velikovsky, orgone energy, Bridey Murphy, medical fads, etc. 373pp.           20394-8 Pa. $3.00

HOAXES, Curtis D. MacDougall. Unbelievably rich account of great hoaxes: Locke's moon hoax, Shakespearean forgeries, Loch Ness monster, Disumbrationist school of art, dozens more; also psychology of hoaxing. 54 illustrations. 338pp.                                                                 20465-0 Pa. $3.50

THE GENTLE ART OF MAKING ENEMIES, James A.M. Whistler. Greatest wit of his day deflates Wilde, Ruskin, Swinburne; strikes back at inane critics, exhibitions. Highly readable classic of impressionist revolution by great painter. Introduction by Alfred Werner. 334pp.                                     21875-9 Pa. $4.00

THE BOOK OF TEA, Kakuzo Okakura. Minor classic of the Orient: entertaining, charming explanation, interpretation of traditional Japanese culture in terms of tea ceremony. Edited by E.F. Bleiler. Total of 94pp.           20070-1 Pa. $1.25